Collaboration

in

Lifelong

Learning

Ministry of Education, Ontario
Information Centre, 13th Floor,
Mowat Block, Queen's Park,
Toronto, Ont.   M7A 1L2

Copyright © 1983 Wendell Smith. All rights reserved. No part of this book may be reproduced in any form or by any electronic or mechanical means including information retrieval systems without permission in writing from the publisher, except by a reviewer who may quote brief pages in a review. Manufactured in the United States of America.

Library of Congress Catalogue Card No.: 83-90997

Smith, Dr. Wendell
Collaboration in Lifelong Learning

ISBN 0-88379-0378

Published by The American Association for Adult and Continuing Education
1201 Sixteenth Street, N.W.
Washington, D.C. 20036
Ph. (202) 822-7866

Contents
   I. **Foreword** / 3
  II. **Introduction** / 7
 III. **Consultants' Position Papers**
   An Opportunity For Cooperation/LLOYD DAVIS / 13
     Synthesis Commentary / 21
   Thoughts on Developing America's Human Resources for the Future/MIKE DOYLE / 25
     Synthesis Commentary / 39
   A Once-In-A-Century Update of the Educational Model/RECK NIEBUHR / 43
     Synthesis Commentary / 50
   A Loosely Coupled System for Adult Education Organizations/THURMAN WHITE / 55
     Synthesis Commentary / 63
     Practice Voting / 64
  IV. **Issues Identification**
   The Issue Identification Process / 65
   List of Twenty-Two Issues / 66
   V. **Issue Resolution Recommendations**
   The Process Utilized to Determine Alternatives to Major Issues / 69
     Issues Analyzed:
   A. Collaborative Effort Among Adult Education Associations and Groups on Legislative Matters Affecting Them/NED LESTER, FACILITATOR / 73
   B. Increasing Awareness of the Importance of Lifelong Learning by the General Public, Educational Institutions and Teachers/MARY GREFE, FACILITATOR / 77

      C. National/Federal Policy on Lifelong Learning/ROGER HIEMSTRA, FACILITATOR / **81**
      D. Restructure and Reallocation of Strategies to Respond to Future and Emerging Technologies/EVERETTE NANCE, FACILITATOR / **85**

VI. **Synthesis / 91**

VII. **Sponsors**

    W. K. Kellogg Foundation / **97**
    The American Association for Adult and Continuing Education / **101**

VIII. **Follow-up plans / 105**

IX. **Appendices**

    A. *Retreat Participants* / **109**
    B. *Composite of Pre-Retreat Participants' Questionnaires* / **112**
    C. *Agenda* / **121**
    D. *Evaluation* / **123**

Collaboration in Lifelong Learning

A Report on the Airlie House
Lifelong Learning Leaders Retreat

Edited by
Wendell L. Smith

Published by
American Association For
Adult and Continuing Education

John Brademas
NEW YORK, NEW YORK

John Brademas became thirteenth President of New York University in July 1981. Before coming to New York, Dr. Brademas served for twenty-two years (1959–81) as United States Representative in Congress from Indiana's Third District, the last four as House Majority Whip, third-ranking member of the Majority Leadership.

While in Congress John Brademas earned a particular reputation for his leadership in education and the arts. In 1975, he was voted one of the nation's four most influential leaders in higher education in a *Change* magazine poll of 4,000 colleges and university presidents, foundation executives, journalists and government officials.

Dr. Brademas has been awarded honorary degrees by twenty-eight colleges and universities, including the City College of New York, Colgate, Tufts, the University of Southern California, the University of Notre Dame, and the Claremont (California) Graduate School.

During twenty-two years of service on the Education and Labor Committee, Dr. Brademas played a principal role in helping write most major legislation concerning elementary and secondary education, higher education, vocational education, services for the elderly and handicapped, and Federal support for libraries, museums and the arts and humanities. He was chief architect of the National Institute of Education, the principal Federal agency supporting research in education, and a major sponsor of the Higher Education Acts of 1972 and 1976.

I. Foreword

We have in recent years witnessed an unprecedented boom in continuing education.

As President of New York University, an institution with a deep commitment to lifelong learning, and as a former member of Congress who sponsored legislation to support education at all levels, I believe that one of the most significant issues facing educators and policymakers today is the phenomenal growth of continuing education. Why do I say this?

There is first an increasing awareness on the part of the American people of the importance of education to our future. More and more Americans are coming to realize that without trained and educated men and women to build the buildings, manage the plants and design the machinery, program the computers and fashion the systems, our country will simply not be able to achieve the renewed economic growth and strong defense posture to which we all aspire.

Second, we live in a time in which sweeping demographic and economic changes are transforming the nature of both work and leisure. It is an era in which information is power, with the amount of new knowledge increasing exponentially. Work has become more complex than ever before and requires more sophisticated job skills. With an economy characterized by a stress on services and rooted in high technology, these skills become obsolete more rapidly. Some estimates hold that in the future people will change jobs four to six times during their careers. In such a society, the need for retraining is obvious.

Still other factors are increasing the demand for lifelong learning programs: the entry of women into the labor force, the aging of our population, the growth in leisure time.

For all these reasons, continuing education is one of the fastest growing areas of higher education. Adults of all ages in every part of the country are seeking the benefits of education. Colleges and universities, beset by economic constraints and declines in traditional full-time enrollments, have rushed to serve this new market of learners.

In my view, the dramatic rise in continuing education presents an exciting opportunity to our educational institutions. But if we are fully to meet the special needs of this heterogeneous population of students, we must address questions of cost, access and quality control. Educators and policymakers must work together to develop coherent strategies to establish a framework for the future of continuing education.

The Lifelong Learning Leaders Retreat, sponsored by the American Association for Adult and Continuing Education and supported by the W. K. Kellogg Foundation, is an important milestone in this process. The meeting last year brought together leaders from twenty organizations concerned with continuing education to identify critical issues and to determine directions for dealing with them.

The report on that retreat both illumines these issues and provides a basis for further analysis.

At a time of resurgent interest in education in this country, I think it imperative that we direct more attention to the role of continuing education and its promise for lifting the level of life for millions of people.

I commend the W. K. Kellogg Foundation for helping place lifelong learning on our national agenda and I highly commend this provocative report.

The Conference Center provided a relaxing atmosphere for participants to live, work and achieve total concentration on the purposes of the retreat.

Wendell Smith
ST. LOUIS, MISSOURI

Dr. Smith has held a variety of teaching and administrative positions in university adult and continuing education; he currently serves as Dean, Continuing Education-Extension, at the University of Missouri-St. Louis, and is responsible for the administration of a program which annually serves over 75,000 adults through non-credit programs and off-campus credit courses.

During the past year, Dr. Smith has been on leave of absence from his university responsibilities while serving as President of the Adult Education Association of the United States (AEA/USA). His responsibilities have encompassed extensive travel to state and regional meetings of AEA affiliate organizations and to annual conferences of allied professional associations.

II. Introduction

Throughout the history of the United States, our societies have engaged in lifelong learning. Initially, the motivation for adult lifelong learning was primarily as a necessity for individual and societal survival; however, today's post-industrial society, due to changes such as increased leisure time and technological advances, has extended a variety of educational opportunities which were never available to our ancestors. Today, lifelong learning is pursued for a variety of reasons, ranging from personal enrichment to increasing job competencies. Lifelong learning is growing at an astonishing rate, both in terms of student participation and in the number and types of providers.

There are approximately 120 million persons 25 years of age or older in our population, and according to the National Center for Education Statistics (NCES), 20 percent (or 24 million) of these adults were involved in a formal learning experience last year. Many view the National Center for Education Statistics data as conservative, and reference even higher participation rates, such as those which were reported at the 1981 National Adult Education Conference. Reported at this conference was a study, conducted by the College Board, which reflected that 60 million adults (or approximately one-half of the population over 25 years of age) had formally learned one or more topics in the past year.

According to NCES, participation in lifelong learning has grown at a 12 percent per annum rate over each of the past five years. By the year 2000, the Census Bureau estimates that nearly 60 percent of our population will be over 30 years of age.

Lifelong learning is a diverse field which transpires in a multitude of settings such as: adult secondary schools' basic literacy programs, vocational and technical education, human resource development training in business and industry and continuing professional education at post-secondary institutions.

As student interest in lifelong learning has increased, there has been a corresponding growth in the number and diversity of national professional associations to which the expanding field relates. These associations typically have the following purposes: (1) to serve as advocates with the general public and with legislators for the particular facet of lifelong learning for adults which they represent; (2) to aid in developing the professional competencies of their members through conferences and publications; (3) to encourage research leading to the further development of the profession; and (4) to serve as a communications link between their members and the members of other associations representing allied concerns.

Although the variety of professional associations has merit in many respects, there is, in many instances, a lack of cooperation which is often evidenced by duplication of services and lack of continuity in legislative relations, research and long-range planning. Such lack of continuity often presents a less than desirable, confusing voice for the profession.

The Planning Processes

Scope of Project

A proposal was developed during the Spring of 1981 by the development committee of the Adult Education Association (now the American Association for Adult and Continuing Education). This proposal, which was subsequently funded by the W. K. Kellogg Foundation, encompassed a three-stage process. Stage I was to include visits between the project director and allied lifelong learning associations to ascertain their interest in participating in the project and to enlist their suggestions concerning possible goals which could be accomplished.

Stage II involved holding a retreat with the chief elected officer and the chief executive official or their representative from major lifelong learning organizations as participants. At the retreat, participants would identify the major issues likely to confront lifelong learners and lifelong learning associations during the next decade. Retreat participants also were to collaboratively consider both individual and collective alternatives which could lead to the resolution of the major issues which were identified.

Stage III of the project was to involve the printing and dissemination of this publication to the retreat participants and other national leaders in lifelong learning. It was hoped that this publication would serve as a blueprint to provide future direction to the lifelong learning movement in the United States.

The Retreat

Objectives: The retreat had four major purposes. These included:
1. Foster better acquaintance among leaders of lifelong learning associations and organizations.
2. Identify major issues which will likely confront lifelong learners and lifelong learning professional associations within the next decade.
3. Analyze alternatives leading to the resolution of major issues which are identified.
4. Formulate recommendations for individual association action and for collaborative efforts between associations.

Participants: Consideration was given to who should be invited to participate in the retreat. Also, special consideration was given to the retreat format and the selection of the retreat location.

An initial list of sixty professional associations which were directly involved in lifelong learning was developed. It was felt that for this initial meeting the more the participating associations had in common, the greater the likelihood would be that the meeting would yield more productive discussions and that follow-up would occur on resolutions which might emerge from the retreat discussions. The list of sixty associations was subsequently reduced to twenty associations which had lifelong learning as their primary mission. This decision was made in order to keep the number of participants to a workable size to help facilitate informal interchange of information and to help foster interpersonal linkages among participants. The twenty associations were each invited to send two representatives to the retreat: (1) the chief elected officer, and (2) the chief executive official, or their respective designee.

Resource Personnel: In an effort to assure that a maximum amount of discussion would transpire among the retreat participants, a small cadre of nonconferees were identified to be in charge of overall functional coordination and administrative logistics at the retreat.

Four consultants were identified in the early stages of the project; their roles were to assist with the overall planning and design of the retreat, to help develop the participant questionnaire and to review the participants' responses, and to develop a cursory position paper referencing major issues and possible collaborative alternatives which would lead to the issues' resolution.

In addition to each presenting a position paper, the consultants interacted informally with participants throughout the retreat.

In an effort to help facilitate small group discussions, four persons were asked to serve as facilitators. In addition to assisting the small groups in identifying issues and formulating recommendations for individual association action and for collaborative efforts among associations, the facilitators kept notes on the major points which were discussed and assisted in presenting the conference closing recommendations.

A synthesizer aided the retreat participants in analyzing recommendations and orchestrating on-site reporting of resolutions which were developed.

In addition to the project director, an administrative secretary, a facilities coordinator and a director of on-site registration represented the balance of the resource personnel.

Retreat Site: The site chosen for the retreat was the Airlie House, which is operated by the Airlie Foundation, a nonprofit corporation. The retreat facilities are located in Airlie, Virginia, which is approximately a one-hour drive from metropolitan Washington, D.C. Since approximately one-half of the retreat participants were based in Washington, D.C., the location of the retreat facility served to minimize travel expenses, yet it was far enough from the participants' offices to discourage the normal office-related interruptions which are often associated with attending a conference in one's home community.

The Retreat Format: In an effort to foster advance consideration of alternatives which could be considered at the retreat, participants were requested to complete a questionnaire. The composite response to the questionnaire (see Appendix B) was shared with all participants prior to the retreat. The responses also served as a basis for the alternatives which were presented in the four consultants' position papers.

Following registration, the conference commenced with a group dinner and a brief overview of the major purposes of the retreat. Participants were asked to introduce themselves and to briefly highlight the respective associations which they were representing.

On the following morning, each of the four consultants provided highlights of his position paper. The participants subsequently divided into four concurrent groups to identify problems and issues which would likely confront the profession in the next decade.

Following lunch, a plenary session was held to allow the participants to react to the issues which had been identified. Through the aid of electronic balloting equipment, the issues were voted upon concerning their relative importance.

Each of the four issues which were viewed as having the greatest importance was subsequently discussed in four concurrent small group settings during the afternoon and evening. Participants were allowed to join the discussion group which dealt with the issue of greater importance to their association. In a plenary session on the final morning of the retreat, the four groups shared the recommendations which they had developed for the issue they discussed. Electronic balloting equipment was again employed in an effort to ascertain the retreat participants' collective views on each of the recommendations which were made.

The retreat concluded with a general synthesis report which was made concerning the total retreat.

Lloyd Davis
GREAT FALLS, VIRGINIA

Dr. Davis has established a distinguished career in the lifelong learning field. He served as Chief Federal Administrator for Cooperative Extension under President Johnson. In this capacity, he provided leadership on Federal policies and gave direction to the outreach programs at land grant universities across the nation.

Dr. Davis served as Executive Director of the National University Continuing Education Association (NUCEA), and later as Interim Executive Director of the Adult Education Association of the United States (AEA/USA).

Dr. Davis is currently President of Davis and Associates, a corporation which provides consulting services in association management and continuing education.

III. Consultants' Position Papers

Four consultants, each representing broad and differing experiences and backgrounds in lifelong learning, reviewed the pre-retreat questionnaires which the participants completed. Based on the questionnaire responses and their personal experience and insights, each consultant developed a position paper on issues in lifelong learning and collaborative alternatives which could lead to their resolution.

The following papers were shared with the participants prior to the retreat and served as the basis for discussions at the opening plenary session.

An Opportunity For Cooperation

In my brief remarks, I will devote my attention to but one of the opportunities for cooperation among the organizations represented here—government and congressional relations. I do this for several reasons: first, because I have had some experience in such cooperation; and second, because I think it is important.

In the past, the needs and interests of adult learners have generally received something less than high priority consideration in the congressional relations of associations that represent the top management of educational institutions, professional schools, state educational agencies, teachers and professors. There are, of course, some exceptions to this, notably the American Association for Community and Junior Colleges (AACJC), which has championed fair and equitable treatment of adult students. Also, we should commend the American Council on Education (ACE) for raising adult learner concerns to a much higher position in its structure. By working together, the associations that have the education and training of adults as their primary concern can raise these concerns to a much higher level in the agenda of these other associations and can have a far greater impact there and in Congress than when going it alone.

Practically all of the respondents to the questionnaire projected increased collaboration among lifelong learning associations on legislative relations, and two-thirds of the respondents said that such collaboration would "increase substantially." This is one of the answers on which there was the highest degree of agreement.

There was an almost equal degree of agreement that the role of government in paying the costs of adult and continuing education will remain the same or decline. There probably would have been a similar response to this last question before Congress amended the Title IV of the Higher Education Act to require that Pell Grants be provided to adult students with dependents on the basis of the same needs test as dependent students, or before Congress passed the recent Job Training Partnership Act with its provisions that permit use of a high proportion of the funds it may provide for training adults. These two pieces of legislation could provide a couple of billion dollars a year of Federal support to education and training of adults.

One could conclude from these answers that we will be getting together to defend the existing level of government support and that we do not expect a high degree of success from our government relations efforts.

I think, however, the answers to these two questions are not necessarily related. I suspect our projections of less government support reflect our recognition of the current public attitude toward reduced roles for government and the current budgetary problems of State and Federal government. I also suspect our projection of increased collaboration on legislative relations reflects a general recognition among us that none of these associations has any excess of political influence and that when several associations work together and present a united front on matters of mutual interest, they can have much greater achievements than when each association goes it alone, and a recognition that in the long run, there are or will be realistic opportunities to increase government support for adult and continuing education and to increase the effectiveness of that support.

I am convinced there are and will be such opportunities. I would like to discuss some of these opportunities, in hopes that this may help generate other ideas and that the process in which we are engaged will contribute to achieving the considerably increased collaboration you project.

In my 25 years in Washington, I have observed that in times of greatest austerity in Federal budgets, there is always some cause, some problem, some need that is receiving increased attention and increased budgets, and that frequently support of some kind of education is or should be an important part of the governmental response. To whit, in this very austere year, the Congress passed the Job Training Partnership Act which Congress is expected to fund to the tune of several billion dollars per year. Also, we might assume that after the next election, there may well be opportunities to launch new program ideas. We should now be developing legislative goals that then might be achieved.

Let me briefly discuss some ideas that might be included in our plans. First, I want to comment on opportunities provided by the Job Training Partnership Act. This Act can prove to be a milestone in Federal support of education and training. Clearly, Congress expects something different from and better than CETA. The Act provides a basis for the development of new kinds of cooperation among business, industry, educational institutions, local government and other groups interested in education and training. This new cooperation could contribute importantly to improving the imperfect linkages between education and work. The Act presents a potential for greatly increased support of education and training for needy adults, for the very groups who have been least well-served by our systems of adult and continuing education.

The Department of Labor must now be working on regulations to implement the Act. The organizations represented here might have an important input in the regulation writing process. I assume that some of these organizations will be cooperating to maximize their input.

A big part of the Act is the provision for state-wide committees to provide policies and supervision for state-administered programs and for similar committees in each service delivery area. Much will depend on the interests, abilities and knowledge of the people appointed to these committees. Let me suggest that the organizations represented here urge their members in each state to start working soon to see to it that competent and knowledgable people are appointed to these committees. This could be one of the most important things we do in the next few months. It is a job on which several organizations might cooperate closely.

About three years ago, when the Higher Education Act was reauthorized, several of these associations formed a coalition dedicated to obtaining amendments to require equitable treatment of adult students (compared to dependent students) in the administration of student aid. We made substantial progress on that objective, at least for the adult student with dependents. More remains to be done. Further progress will be difficult under the present budgetary situation. But I hope you do not abandon the cause.

Also, several associations here have worked to eliminate IRS rules under which educational and training costs paid by employers were treated for tax purposes as income to the person who received the training. Maintaining present rules will require continued vigilance. I would suggest that there is more to be done on the tax front. Under current rules, if an individual obtains education and training for use in his present job, the cost is a tax deduction. If he obtains education and training to prepare for another job in which he would be more productive, the cost is not deductible. There is no logic to this, particularly when our economy is crying for increased productivity. I hope you take on this inequity as a cause.

It is just a matter of time before Congress passes a new veterans' training act. We might anticipate that when unemployment rates go down, so will enlistments and that then the Congress will move a new veterans' training act to the front burner. Some of you probably have been involved in the drafting of such bills now before Congress. It might be helpful if others represented here joined with you in helping to build and support such legislation.

One important lesson from the past is that Congress has provided funds for adult and continuing education for segments of the populations as a means of achieving particular objectives or missions of agencies of the Federal government. Veterans' education initially was a means of helping veterans adjust to civilian life. The Law Enforcement Education Program was a means of improving law enforcement. Co-op extension is a means of improving the quality of farm and rural life. The Adult Education Act is directed at reducing illiteracy and making some people more employable.

In almost every agency of government, there are one or more programs in which funds are or may be used for some kind of education or training for some group of adults related to achieving the missions of that agency. But in most cases, the funds are very limited and the role of education is likewise limited. In general, the vision and understanding of the role that education might play in achieving agency goals held by Federal program administrators is perhaps the critical factor limiting agency support of educational activity.

For example, out of the nearly one billion a year spent by the National Science Foundation, only a pittance is spent to encourage the application of research results, under such labels as "Science for Citizens," and "Technology Transfer." This at a time when our economy is crying for the increased productivity that the application of research results could help provide. Those of us who have worked to encourage people to apply the results of research know that educational processes greatly increase the rate of application. People apply research results when they understand the results, understand how the results can help them, have the skills required and have confidence they can make the application with a high probability of benefits and low probability of loss, and when they know the magnitude of the potential benefits in terms of achieving their goals. Carefully planned educational efforts can provide this knowledge and understanding. Yet research workers and administrators think mainly in terms of publishing research results in learned journals.

Another example, very briefly: my son-in-law is involved in the administration of a Federal flood insurance program. He observed that one of his greatest problems was the lack of knowledge among officials of local government of flood hazards and the kinds of action that might reduce these hazards. He proposed an educational program to improve the knowledge of local officials in this area to be funded from discretionary funds of the agency and to be conducted by a local educational institution. After several years, the agency is beginning to recognize that education for local officials and leading citizens will help it achieve its goals.

I am convinced that there are many opportunities for increasing government support of adult and continuing education to aid in achieving the missions of government agencies. I am further convinced that such expenditures can greatly increase the efficiency and effectiveness with which government agencies pursue the goals and missions provided them by the Congress. Such educational programs must be carefully designed and targeted and must apply a variety of education techniques and media in strategies designed to achieve their objectives.

As we look to possible future governmental support, we should propose educational roles related to *important national* needs. We should propose specific goals for the educational activities and specific population groups as the target audiences. Furthermore, we should be looking into the future, anticipating the issues and needs that are likely to gain high priority attention in a few years. We ought to find pilot programs that illustrate the effectiveness of the proposed educational activities and use these to support our proposed programs.

Here are just a few suggestions we might consider:

The lagging productivity of our American industry is a very important factor behind our economic problems: inflation, excess of imports over exports, unemployment. Proposals for government to do more to attack the productivity problem are likely to receive serious consideration in the Congress soon. As a part of such proposals, we might propose educational programs to speed up the rate at which new cost-cutting technology is applied, to encourage more effective management techniques, to upgrade skills of workers and to affect other factors inhibiting productivity.

We could think about the role of education with respect to the continuing world energy problems, the pending crisis in water supply in the U.S., environmental problems, control of crime, housing problems and many others.

I think one of the greatest needs for public education is with respect to public policy. As our world gets increasingly complex and public policy issues increasingly involve highly technical questions, we tend to rely to a greater extent on the judgments of technical experts in the formulation of policy, and individual citizens have difficulty formulating sound judgments and expressing them through our political processes. Yet such participation by citizens is vital to our system of government. I believe there is a critical need for educational systems through which citizens may obtain objective analysis of policy alternatives and learn to express their judgments effectively. You may be aware that David Matthews, ex-secretary of HEW, is much concerned about this need and has developed a new organization to address it.

On the surface, it appears as though this is a need government cannot finance, even though it may be essential to preserving our form of government. The administration in power almost always has a position on major policy issues, a position it works hard to sell to the public. Few agency heads are willing to encourage public debate that may increase public support of policies that are contrary to the ones they are promoting. But the public knows this and has little respect for the objectivity of government agencies in such issues. Probably educational institutions, among all the institutions in our society, have the greatest reputation for objectivity and are in the best position for leadership in such education. In spite of this limitation on government, the Department of Agriculture does fund objective education on agricultural public policy issues through the Cooperative Extension Service. As Administrator of the Extension Service of USDA, I had some interesting experiences trying to maintain objectivity by a staff in 3,000 counties at a time when the Secretary and farm organizations were arrayed on different sides of a red hot policy issue.

We do have government financing other independent and objective programs that at times may seem to be in conflict with administration policy, for example, NSF and the Federal Reserve. This suggests that there may be a new way to provide government support for this and other educational programs in which there is a national interest.

For example, several years ago, I conceived of an agency parallel to NSF that would have a responsibility for funding public educational programs in the national interest. This could include programs of "technology transfer" to encourage application of research results, public policy education, and other programs related to national problems and needs. Such an agency might have funds to allocate directly to educational organizations, some of which might be used in conjunction with government agencies on programs related to the missions of such agencies.

We sold the idea to President Lyndon Johnson. He referred it to his Commissioner of Education and there the idea died. But this idea, with modifications, could have merit at some time in the future. So, I give you the idea without charge.

Each of our associations has developed some objectives for developing government support for the education of adults in the future, based on the unique roles of the various associations and interests of their members. If each association were to do its own dreaming and planning and then we were to pool our ideas, I suspect we would find much in common. I suspect also we could develop an agenda that we all could support that we could sell to other associations and that would command public respect.

There is a history of cooperative legislative effort among some of the associations represented here, sometimes through the American Council on Education framework, sometimes through informal coalitions that come together for specific purposes. One of the most effective of the informal coalitions was about five years ago when we did battle over legislation to eliminate regulations imposed by the Veterans Administration. We had coalition within coalition to give special attention to special problems. There was a very high degree of cooperation and coordination and we achieved most of our goals.

Another very effective coalition was operating three years ago when we were working to obtain provisions in Title IV of the

Higher Education Act to assure equitable treatment for adult students in student aid programs. Within this informal coalition was a formally organized coalition, CAPE. Again, we had a high degree of coordination among associations. We achieved a large part of our objectives.

These informal coalitions generally form when someone recognizes a specific need for groups to work together and someone takes the initiative to call a meeting, and then when the several parties see such a coalition as being in their self-interest. For the process to work, there must be mutual respect and a desire to achieve a goal sufficiently strong for the participants to be willing to share the credit.

As we look to the future, we might well give attention to ways that the processes by which collaboration in government relations among associations that have a primary interest in the education of adults can be improved. Let me suggest this as an item for your agenda.

Synthesis Comments on Lloyd Davis' Position Paper

Lloyd Davis' paper, I think it's fair to say, spoke most directly to the single most favored kind of future collaboration which conference participants indicated on the pre-conference questionnaire. His reflections and his superbly savvy advice is the best example I've ever seen of the kind of learning—indeed, let's not be afraid to use the term wisdom—which a fine mind can winnow out of a lifetime's experience and submit as a great gift to others in the field. I cannot imagine a better agenda for legislative cooperation than the one he outlines, nor a better strategy for achieving such goals than the ones he suggests, nor a bolder set of fresh initiatives to propose.

I was particularly impressed myself by his recommendation regarding adult education to put the results of research into practice —the idea which he and others sold to Lyndon Johnson, but which then died, as have so many brave notions, in the interstices of the Federal education bureaucracy.

> . . . One important lesson from the past is that Congress has provided funds for adult and continuing education for segments of the

populations as a means of achieving particular objectives or missions of agencies of the Federal government. Veterans' education initially was a means of helping veterans adjust to civilian life. The Law Enforcement Education Program was a means of improving law enforcement. Co-op extension is a means of improving the quality of farm and rural life. The Adult Education Act is directed at reducing illiteracy and making some people more employable.

In almost every agency of government, there is one or more programs in which funds are or may be used for some kind of education or training for some group of adults related to achieving the missions of that agency. But in most cases, the funds are very limited and the role of education is likewise limited. In general, the vision and understanding of the role that education might play in achieving agency goals held by Federal program administrators is perhaps the critical factor limiting agency support of educational activity. . . .

Carefully planned educational efforts can provide this knowledge and understanding. Yet research workers and administrators think mainly in terms of publishing research results in learned journals. . . .

This challenge of making our scientific, educational and academic establishment responsive to public needs and concerns broadly conceived is one that has bedeviled me for fifteen years, in my associations with foundations in fields ranging from biomedical research, through my time at the Ford Foundation, to my present association with the Fund for the Improvement of Postsecondary Education's Mina Shaughnessy Program. We simply must find means for making the life of the mind relevant to, and accessible for, as many Americans as possible—certainly, for far more than now perceive themselves part of it. I can't think of a nobler mission for adult education.

Consultants and Group Facilitators
Left to Right: Lloyd Davis, Consultant, AAACE; Thurman White, Vice Chancellor for Outreach, Oklahoma Regents for Higher Education; Herman (Reck) Niebuhr, Associate Vice President and Assistant to the President, Temple University; Ned Lester, Associate Dean, Virginia Polytechnical Institute and State University; Mary Grefe, President of Lead Associates, Ltd. (Des Moines); Wendell Smith, Dean, Continuing Education-Extension, University of Missouri-St. Louis; Everette Nance, Associate Professor of Education Administration and Director, Community Education Development Center, University of Missouri-St. Louis; Ron Gross, Director of the Independent Scholarship Project and Senior Consultant to the College Board (Dr. Gross was the Retreat conference synthesizer and reporter); Michael Doyle, Senior Associate and co-founder of Interaction Associates, Inc. (San Francisco); Roger Hiemstra, Professor and Program Leader—Adult Studies, Syracuse University.

Michael Doyle
SAN FRANCISCO, CALIFORNIA

Michael Doyle is Senior Associate with and co-founder of Interaction Associates, Inc. For the past ten years he has focused on improving the productivity of organizations and urban areas utilizing collaborative planning and decision-making strategies. He serves as a neutral facilitator and consultant with many boards of directors for private sector organizations.

He has trained people in a wide variety of applied behavioral science methodologies, including meeting effectiveness, board effectiveness, problem-solving, decision-making, communications, planning, organizational development, inter-agency collaboration, conflict resolution, citizen involvement, leadership and training of trainers.

Michael Doyle is co-author with David Straus of the best-selling book, *How To Make Meetings Work*, Wyden Books, 1976, and Playboy Press, 1977. He is featured in the New Visucom Productions' management training film, *Meetings: Isn't There A Better Way?* He has also authored and co-authored many articles on collaborative problem-solving and process management.

The following position paper was developed by Mike Doyle and two associates of his firm, Interaction Associates, Inc.; Sarah L. Dunmeyer, Research Intern, and Margi Dunlap, Writer/Consultant.

Thoughts on Developing America's Human Resources For The Future

"The most sweeping changes in the working world since the industrial revolution worry many Americans," stated a recent newspaper article in the *Dallas Morning News*. It quoted a recent national survey by ITT Education Services, Inc. which concluded, *"four out of five people doubt they have the skills to hold jobs in the labor market of the future."*

To me that's a rather startling statistic—that predicts both crisis and opportunity for our society—especially for our educational institutions and businesses.

I'm glad to have the opportunity to prepare this conference paper. It's given me an opportunity to articulate thoughts that have been incubating in recent years. Working mainly in the private sector for the past twelve years as a collaborative systems design and human resource consultant, I've had the good fortune to be able to design and participate in many large-scale organizational change and renewal efforts. These efforts always include giving people in those organizations the skills and knowledge to conduct their business in new ways. The projects have given me opportunities to observe firsthand some of the activities that are contributing to the beginning of a *human resource development renaissance of unprecedented scale* in corporate America today.

My paper addresses four main areas:
1. An environmental scan of the social, economic and demographic trends affecting human resources development/lifelong learning today.
2. Corporate and organizational initiatives.
3. Analysis and implications.
4. General conclusions for the human resources development/ lifelong learning community.

Environmental Scan

Social, Demographic and Economic Trends. The pace of social change in this country has been quickened by quantum leaps of technology in the last decade. The introduction of new technologies such as personal computers, electronic mail, teleconferencing, robotics, electronic banking, data banks and bases is happening and will continue to happen on an enormous scale. With its concurrent upheaval, I witness frequently the organizational computer wars between the "mini" and "mainframe" enthusiasts. John Naisbett, in *Megatrends*, calls our time an "information age" which, in the future, will be viewed as significant a revolution as the industrial revolution was in its time. In 1950, only about 17% of us worked in information type jobs. Today, most Americans spend their work time creating, processing or distributing information. Now, only 13% of California's labor force is engaged in manufacturing operations. Other estimates vary, but the fact remains. We are no longer and never will be again an industrial society. We have shifted to an information society based on knowledge and services.

Who works in this information economy? The demographics are fascinating. We—all of us—are getting older. In 1975, the average worker was 28. In 1990, the average worker will be 40, and there won't be very many high school age youths to fill entry level slots in anyone's business. Julie O'Mara, 1983 American Society for Training and Development's President-Elect, predicts in her paper, "Combating the Human Capital Crisis," that the conflict between the "baby boomers" of post-World War II and the "baby busters" of the 1970's will cause a bottleneck at the tops of organizations, fierce competition for the new job seekers, and a severe crisis in Social Security funding by the late 1980's. Two-thirds of the new entrants to the workforce will be women. According to a new government study, the number of women working in the United States has already risen 21 million or 95 percent over the last two decades. Many of the jobs they hold are in categories once largely the province of men. By 1988, fully one-fourth of our population will be Hispanics and Blacks. How will our organizational cultures change to take this greater diversity into account? A replay of the '60's? Most challenging of all, Peter Drucker, a leading management theorist, predicts that up to 15 million jobs in manufacturing will become obsolete in the next decade. On the bright(?) side, a quarter of a million new jobs will be created in high technology fields, like electrical engineering, electronics and computers. But what about the other 14¾ million people who will need something new to do?

In spite of these uncertainties, the working population is making new demands. The "organization man" of the fifties no longer exists. As technology advances, human needs are being represented with equal eloquence. Workers are demanding broader participation in the decisions that affect their lives. Networks are beginning to replace hierarchies. Flextime, paternity leaves, job-sharing, employee involvement programs, Theory Z, job rotation, participative management and (most significant for us) job retraining and job redesign are all becoming part of the package that businesses must put together to maintain and retain a valued workforce. Look at Silicon Valley, the home of the computer revolution in California. Worker allegiance is shifting from the organization to "the technology." Workers are migrating to work on "the latest development in their field" regardless of its organizational context. People in the labor force are making demands about the quality of their own work lives and those demands are being heard.

A full 73% of our population believes that they have more freedom of choice than their parents did. This is a hopeful statistic, though it indicates a profound social and cultural change to be made in only a generation. On the hopeful side, Daniel Yankelovich, in his book *New Rules: Search for Fulfillment in a World Turned Upside Down,* believes this demand for choice is being manifest in a broader tolerance for cultural diversity, a richer form of self expression in the arts, more creative individualism in education and religion and an increased responsiveness in the market place.

Businesses are now asking "How do you design organizational cultures that make the people feel welcome, creative and productive?" More importantly, "How do you teach managers to manage them effectively?"

In addition to demographic and social trends, two economic trends will have a profound impact on our society, on how we develop our human resources and how we all learn through our whole lives.

We are clearly shifting from an industrial to an information-based service economy. Industrial production will move to the third world. In 1960, the U.S. accounted for 26% of worldwide steel production. Today, it is only 14% and shrinking. In that same period, Japan has increased its share from 6.4% to 15.5% and production in the developing world rose from 39.3% to 52.6%. U.S. Representative James Blanchard, D-Michigan, recently elected governor and sponsor of the Chrysler Loan Guarantee bill, known colloquially as "The Chrysler Bail Out Bill," that provided the company with $1.5 billion in Federally backed loans, recently stated: "The issue right now is whether we will be able to save our industrial base, and if we are, how much of it we will save. It is not whether we will save all of it . . . it is a crisis which threatens to leave our auto industry permanently diminished by one-half, and our steel, rubber and glass industries dramatically reduced in scale."

Due to technology and worldwide competition, we are shifting from a national to a global economy. Philip Caldwell, Chairman of Ford Motor Company, has said, "Our relative position in the world has changed because the seeds we planted around the world took root and the seeds now have become mature trees, so to speak. Just consider this: as recently as 1967, the United States built more motor vehicles than the rest of the world combined. That was only 15 years ago. Japan was number one in production last year, and Europe was number two." These massive changes are having a substantial impact on our near-term economic and human resource futures as a nation. We, as a society, need to come to grips with these issues with clearly articulated long-range, comprehensive, future development scenarios and policies and get out of our reactive mode. Should we erect tariffs to protect our industrial base or develop policies to speed the shift to a service, high-technology base? In the November 21st *San Francisco Chronicle*, a front page article stated, "President Reagan sought Saturday to still growing demands for protection of domestic industries in the United States and Europe, saying that government restrictions on free trade ultimately posed a threat to peace. 'Free trade serves the cause of economic progress, and it serves the cause of world peace,' the President said. 'When governments get too involved in trade, economic costs increase and political disputes multiply. Peace is threatened.' "

How is it that the associations represented in this room are not in the thick of this debate with clearly articulated positions? These trends portend a major shift in America's position vis-a-vis the world—both politically and economically. They will have a profound impact on our society, our mind sets and our institutions. These major shifts in demographics, social and economic trends and our economic base forecast major implications for the educational community. They will change our world view and the fabric of our society. They will alter the shape of our work, the way we work and the way we think about work. Our corporations, institutions of higher learning and we, as individuals, need to prepare for these shifts NOW.

Corporate and Community Responses

The trends described above are going to continue to fundamentally change the way corporate America conducts business, and change the way it views its most vital resources. In a low margin, low growth service economy, people—our human resources—are taking on an importance equal to or greater than capital and equipment combined. Corporate America knows this and is adapting to these unprecedented changes in the marketplace.

Consider this: Businesses and corporations spend about $36 billion a year on training. To put this into perspective, or rather to compare it to something, the University of California, which is the largest educational institution in the world, had an annual budget for 1982 of $3.8 billion, less than one-eighth of the amount spent by the private sector. American Telephone and Telegraph, which was (before it got dismantled) the largest corporation on earth, has a training budget of $1.7 billion, and close to 10,000 people employed as trainers for 12,000 courses in 1,300 locations. Just to check out a curiosity of mine—Do you include those ten thousand AT&T trainers in your own minds as part of your peer group, your network?

Consider also for a moment the half-life of today's technical educations. M.I.T. Electrical Engineering Professor Louis Smullin stated in the October 18 issue of *Time Magazine*, "Engineers are washed up by the time they are 35 or 40, and new ones are recruited from the universities." The article continues, "Each year some 10,000, or 5%, of the nation's electrical engineers transfer out of their field, many because they feel useless or technologically obsolete. Yet, by 1985, the U.S. is expected to suffer from a shortage of more than 100,000 engineers. This gap cannot be closed by increasing the output of engineering schools, which are at their production limit. As Ray Stata, president of Analog Devices, told an M.I.T. symposium, 'Our only viable strategy for coping is for industry to increase the productivity, retention and competence of those engineers already engaged in the profession.' "

The committee concluded, "The problems we are facing cannot be solved simply by incrementally improving and expanding current educational programs. A quantum jump is needed, amounting to a revolution in engineering education." The committee proposed a new alliance between industry and academe under which, on company time and at company expense, engineers would continue their graduate-level education in at least one 15-week course per year. Universities should adopt residency requirements flexible enough so that graduate-level courses could be taught at the workplace. It recommended that as much as 10% of engineers' working time be devoted to continuing education for the duration of their working lives!

Corporations are changing their attitudes toward what ASTD's Julie O'Mara calls "human capital." They feel it is one of the most important investments they can make—at least as important as plant maintenance and machinery. When I started consulting and training twelve years ago, many training departments were far removed from the executive suite and wielded little power. In a recent study of Texas corporations, 54% placed the training function no more than one reporting level from the Chief Executive Officer and

74% said they have increased their training budgets over the previous year.

Findings from a survey of 125 training directors in Fortune 500 corporations and fast-growing smaller companies, commissioned by Sandy Corporation in Southfield, Michigan, show that 79% expect their training budgets to increase during the next five years, regardless of economic conditions. Fifteen percent expect their budget to double.

Look at the membership in the American Society for Training and Development (ASTD) which has doubled in size since 1976. Currently, its 132 local chapters and national memberships total over 50,000. ASTD attributes its growth to an increasing awareness by corporations of the importance of training and development to the productivity of their organization. Yet, the current ASTD president, Ed Scannel, feels that this growth represents less than one tenth of the potential membership based on ASTD's estimates of the field.

The Five Major Corporate Renewal Thrusts in This Decade

Corporations are using five major change strategies to cope with these new trends and maintain or regain their competitive edge. All have major human resource implications. These strategies are:
- Technological
- Structural
- Procedural
- Individual
- Combination

These strategies are based on the assumption that corporations will not be able to carry on business as usual and that mere retrenchment will not allow them to continue to build innovative and profitable future institutions.

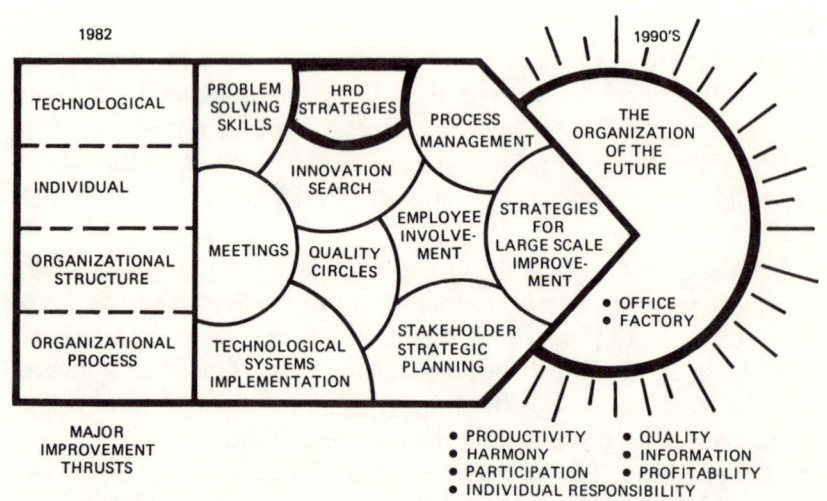

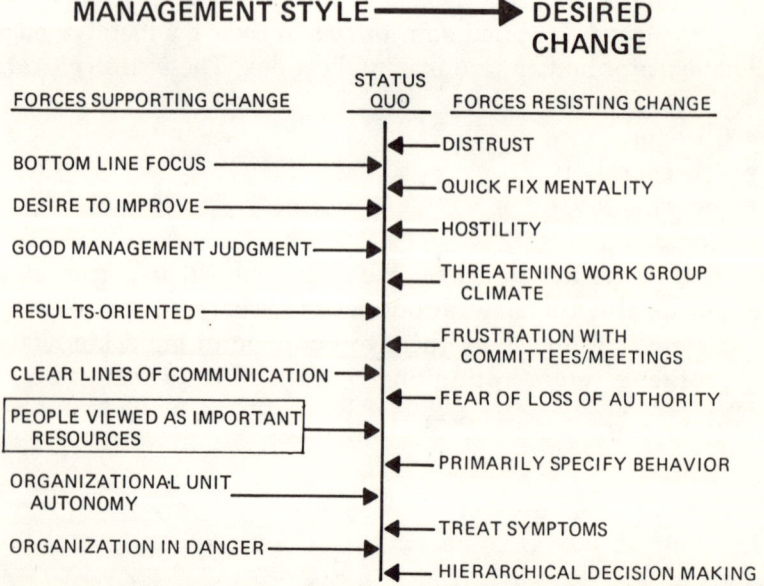

Technological Strategies: Corporations are introducing new technologies into their organizations on an unprecedented scale. Robots, computer control and data-processing systems, computer-aided design and computer-aided manufacturing (CAD/CAM), electronic mail, personal computers, word processing and teleconferencing are very popular, and there are many more. All are exerting a profound effect on the organizational, social and physical architecture of American business.

Structural Strategies: Another major strategy is to change organizational structures in order to increase responsiveness, flexibility and productivity. Options being tested include matrix designs, both centralized and decentralized systems, work redesigns, and social-technical designs. Organizations are establishing profit centers, networks and self-managed work teams.

Procedural Strategies: Strategies for changing organizational processes are the kind I find myself involved with most often. I describe it as fundamentally altering the "basic process architecture" of the corporation and creating a "parallel process architecture of change and renewal." Moving organizational cultures from adversarial to collaborative environments is a key thrust in many corporations today. Quality Circles, Quality of Work Life programs, consensus decision-making, conflict resolution teams, task forces, gain sharing, problem-solving teams, Pokayoke and Just-In-Time procedures (borrowed from the Japanese) and parallel organizations are being used to improve the "how" in corporations throughout the United States.

Individual Strategies: To cope with these massive changes, employees are being trained in massive numbers to adapt. Managers are being trained in the new technologies both behavioral and technical. Ongoing technical training is becoming a way of life for professional and technical specialists. Process training, facilitation, communication, process management and behavioral change competencies are requisite skills for both managers and supervisors who want to successfully implement these new, more participative, organizational strategies for effectively managing the workers of the 1980's.

My Analysis

As we have seen, profound pressures are changing the nature of work and the workforce. Public and private responses to these pressures often fall short of the vision, magnitude and coordination necessary to retrain 15 million people, prepare the 12 million who will enter the workforce in the 1980's and keep the millions who are currently employed on top of contemporary knowledge and skills.

There are substantial barriers to the U.S. solving these key problems. From the perspective of your university based institutions I perceive these barriers to be:
- lack of a comprehensive overview of trends
- lack of an adequate data base
- all the players are not in the room or playing on the same team
- no common semantic framework
- competition among institutions, products and services
- no agreement on the problem(s)
- no agreement on what should be done or how to do it
- system fragmentation

First and foremost, I wholeheartedly agree with Reck Niebuhr of Temple University. We must get to the root of the real problems from a macro prospective. This probably means setting up a broadly based process think tank to conceptualize both the process of learning, and our institutions of learning, not just the "higher institutions." This can provide us with a comprehensive overview of the system.

We, as educators of adults, must expand our data base if we are to benefit from any of these facts and figures. ASTD tried recently to put together some data on training functions in the private sector. They ran into problems in collecting data because of inconsistencies in the way corporations define "trainer," "training" and "training expenses." The American Society of Association Executives has stated that 83% of its 6,000 member groups offer continuing education activities, and 400 of the associations have a full-time education director. Although there are problems with gathering reliable data, I have a strong hunch that as little as one-half of the adult education in the United States is being provided by schools and colleges. I know it also takes place in industry, the government and the military. Only a conscientious expansion of our own data base can provide us with the information we need to substantiate our claims that "learning" must be redefined in a way that encompasses the whole field.

We in adult education need a common semantic framework. In my work, we preface all of our problem-solving efforts with the belief that in order to solve a problem, you have to agree on the definition of the problem. If, when we're trying to collect data about private sector training, we can't agree on what a trainer is, then we can't collect any credible data.

Is our field "Lifelong Learning," "Adult Education," "Human Resource Development," "Training," or "Human Capital"? I can't even agree with you on a name for what we do, though by now you probably know we do some of the same things. You call it "lifelong learning," which has a personal connotation and implies a continuous process. I prefer "human resources development" because it connotes a policy and planning orientation. We need an umbrella term that encompasses the field, that we can agree on, that means giving adults the skills and knowledge they need to accomplish their life and organizational tasks as effectively as possible, both today and in the future. That's what I mean by a common semantic framework. As business and academia interact to begin to resolve the problems I've outlined in this paper, we need to speak the same language or we'll miss important parts of the communication. We'll end up competing when we could be collaborating to produce better solutions, which brings me to the last thing I want to talk to you about today:

How do we put all this together?

I've noticed an interesting dynamic in my work with organizational systems. When there is a win/lose conflict between two subsystems, the larger system discounts the subsystems and all subsystems in the conflict usually lose in the long term. As an example, throughout the 1970's in elementary and secondary education, conflicts between parents, teachers and administrators have been a major contributing factor to loss of support and funding from the larger system: the society. Unrest, disunity, and lack of clearly supported goals have hurt all parties. Let's not let that happen here.

General Conclusions

As we face the challenges outlined above, it's my conclusion that the problems are so large that no one can solve them alone or use traditional means and mindsets. If we want to have any impact, we need to take an innovative approach and work together on a large scale to reach a fundamental consensus. To achieve this broad-based consensus we need to work together to:

- establish a broadly based process think tank that would promote collaborative efforts within a much broader consortium of Education/LLL/HRD groups than are represented here
- establish as part of the think tank effort strong initiatives between other policy disciplines in the federal government, such as economics and national and foreign policy disciplines, and the Education/LLL/HRD community
- collect data
- agree on the major problems
- develop a common semantic framework
- change the attitudes of individuals toward their own learning and re-education
- promote major investments in human capital by the government, labor and corporate sectors of the economy.

Fantasizing for a bit, I see some of the conclusions such a process might reach:

- merging the Federal Departments of Labor and Education (old paradigms) into a Department of Human Resource Development
- development of a national Human Resource policy
- recommendation that 10% of people's adult working life be committed to learning
- embracing telecommunications technology by launching of the first multi-channel national collaborative televersity
- reconceptualizing our institutions of learning from physical centers ("citadels of knowledge") to facilitators of lifelong developmental and learning processes.

Elements of Successful Collaborative Planning Efforts

Even if you wanted to, how could you make a collaborative effort of this magnitude work expeditiously and effectively? Too many collaborative efforts fail to bear fruit because we don't understand the social technology needed to make them work. I think, based on my firm's ten years of action research, that success is possible only when sufficient attention is paid to creating flexible planning process designs that facilitate collaboration. Specifically, I think a collaborative effort of this magnitude must utilize the following principles as guidelines for its own design:

- A collaborative planning process must include from the beginning all the individuals or groups that are responsible for final decisions or affected by the decision. Who are the key stakeholders?
- If you don't agree on the problem, you'll never agree on the solution. Collaborative problem solving is problem oriented vs. solution oriented. What problem(s) do we need to promptly address?
- Participants in a collaborative process must own the process. They must be involved in designing the process from the beginning.
- The power of collaborative process comes from inclusion, not exclusion. The power of your recommendations will result from the overlapping memberships of the participants. The process should have no formal authority. It is based on consensus of the appropriate stakeholders.
- Participants in this collaborative process should represent points of view and interests, not numbers of people. Participants must be able to increase or decrease their level of involvement through the life of a planning process.
- The commitment of the key decision-making organizations must be evidenced by a commitment of resources (dollars, in-kind support services, personnel, etc.).
- A collaborative process must be educational, open and visible, and seen as ongoing, not as a one-shot deal.

Lastly, the final keys to large-scale successful collaborative efforts are neutrality and accountability. There is no such thing as a neutral planning agency, for once there is a plan, the neutrality becomes compromised. What is needed is a coordinating mechanism with no investment in content outcomes. This mechanism does not speak, but facilitates and encourages the primary players to speak with one voice.

In conclusion, the only way we are going to attack these trends successfully is with vision, a macro perspective and a national collaborative effort on a scale only known before in wartime in this country.

References
1. Anderson, Richard E., "Problems of Collecting Financial Data for Adult Education and Training;" paper prepared for the ASTD Conference, "The Nature and Extent of Employee Training and Development," Washington, D.C., October, 1982.
2. Craig, Robert L., and Evers, Christine, "Employers as Educators: The Shadow System;" Chapter 2 from *Business and Higher Education: Toward New Alliances*, ed. by G.G. Gold, Jossey-Bass Publishers, San Francisco, CA, 1981.
3. Doyle, Michael, and Kraus, William, "Managing Change: Creating the Organization of the Future;" unpublished paper, Interaction Associates, San Francisco, CA, 1982.
4. Jones, Philip, and Zemke, Ron, "Training Magazines Experiences in Gathering Data on Training and Employee Development in Organizational America;" prepared for the ASTD Conference, "The Nature and Extent of Employee Training and Development," Washington, D.C., October, 1982.
5. Naisbett, John, *Megatrends: Ten New Directions Transforming Our Lives;* Warner Books, New York, NY, 1982.
6. O'Mara, Julie, and Berberich, Lynn, "Combating the Human Capital Crisis: Trends and Projections in Human Resources Development;" ASTD, Summer, 1982.
7. Schindler-Rainman, Eva, "Risks We Must Take;" *Training and Development Journal*, August, 1981.
8. Yankelovich, Daniel, *New Rules: Search for Self Fulfillment*

in a World Turned Upside Down; Random House, New York, NY, 1981.
9. Zemke, Ron, "U.S. Training Census and Trends Report, 1982;" *Training/ HRD,* October, 1982.
10. National Report for Training and Development; August 20, 1982, September 29, 1982, and October 28, 1982, issues.
11. Time Magazine, "Computers," October 18, 1982.

Synthesis Comments on Michael Doyle's Position Paper

This meeting has generated the makings of numerous new alliances. But perhaps the grandest of all these alliances is the one Mike Doyle invites us to forge in his consultants' position paper on human resources development. I believe that the alliance he proposes there, between the lifelong learning movement in education and the human resources development movement in the corporate sector, has tremendous economic implications for the field. I also believe it has unique political appeal in our present ideological climate. The kinds of specific plans and programs which it suggests would have the kind of appeal which Lloyd Davis urged us to look for—the kind of plans which might win fresh funding even in a time of general budgetary cutbacks.

Mike is telling us that business and industry are discovering that *people matter* as never before in our economic history. Not just in a sentimental sense, but in dollars, at the bottom line. It is the quality and knowledge and resourcefulness and dedication of people which will be crucial for productivity and for profits in the years just ahead. Mike calls it tellingly, a "human resources development renaissance of unprecedented scale in corporate America today." And, graciously, he invites us to join his renaissance.

> . . . Corporations are changing their attidues toward . . . human capital. They feel it is one of the most important investments they can make—at least as important as plant maintenance and machinery. When I started consulting and training twelve years ago, many training departments were far removed from the executive

suite and wielded little power. In a recent study of Texas corporations, 54% placed the training function no more than one reporting level from the Chief Executive Officer and 74% said they have increased their training budgets over the previous year.

Findings from a survey of 125 training directors in Fortune 500 corporations and fast-growing smaller companies, commissioned by Sandy Corporation in Southfield, Michigan, show that 79% expect their training budgets to increase during the next five years, regardless of economic conditions. Fifteen percent expect their budget to double. . . .

But there's an entry fee to enter this renaissance, Mike warns us. And it goes beyond the need to cut a deal with a corporate client for some training, or crank up another certificate program in word processing. It involves changing our ideas, our concepts, our view of our field. "Learning must be redefined in a way that encompasses the whole field," Mike contends.

> . . . You call it 'lifelong learning,' which has a personal connotation and implies a continuous process. I prefer 'human resources development' because it connotes a policy and planning orientation. We need an umbrella term that encompasses the field, that we can agree on, that means giving adults the skills and knowledge they need to accomplish their life and organizational tasks as effectively as possible, both today and tomorrow. . . .

I'm not so sure myself that a common term or label is as important as the operational alliance which Mike proposes. What's important is that we roll up our sleeves and get to work with corporate America, not just on a piecemeal approach to meeting the needs of business and industry, but on the tasks which Mike outlines. To forge a grand alliance, we need to:

- establish a broadly based process think tank that would promote collaborative efforts within a much broader consortium of Education/LLL/HRD groups than are represented here
- establish as part of the think tank effort strong initiatives between other policy disciplines in the federal government, such as economics and national and foreign policy disciplines, and the Education/LLL/HRD community
- collect data

- agree on the major problems
- develop a common semantic framework
- change the attitudes of individuals towards their own learning and re-education
- promote major investments in human capital by the government, labor and corporate sectors of the economy.

Herman (Reck) Niebuhr, Jr.
PHILADELPHIA, PENNSYLVANIA

Dr. Niebuhr began his career as a clinical psychologist with the School of Medicine at Temple University. Later, he served in an "urbanist" capacity through which he directed a variety of programs for the University which were designed to reach lower socio-economic communities in Philadelphia.

Dr. Niebuhr's current position is Associate Vice President and Assistant to the President for Planning Coordination at Temple University. Work in his current position has encompassed a variety of coordinative programs among post-secondary educational institutions in Pennsylvania. Through his involvement in the Delaware Valley Regional Planning Council for Higher Education, Dr. Niebuhr is responsible for the nationally recognized CLEO project.

A Once-In-A-Century Update of the Educational Model
A Pressing Task for Lifelong Learning Leaders

The Changing Environment

As the pre-retreat questionnaire responses indicated, lifelong learning leaders are aware that they live in a fast-changing environment to which educators must shape a timely and effective response. They are aware that:
- Robert Huchins' metaphor of the nation as a "learning society" is a reality. Lifelong learning is instrumental to meeting the changing challenges and aspirations of our personal, social and economic lives in the years ahead. This leads to optimism that the domain of education, whether in school, college, business, media, etc., has a significant role to play.
- The economic transformation required to make the nation competitive in the international context will require us all to "work smarter." Hence, the renewed partnership between education providers is on everyone's mind. The convergence between educational and business interests is in sharp contrast to the divergence of the 60's, and recalls the climate a century ago when the requirements of the evolving mass industrial economy led to the invention of the land grant institution, the urban colleges and the introduction of vocational education into public education.
- The current educational delivery systems will be obsolete in the computer and telecommunications age. There is a beginning awareness that new organizational inventions, such as joint ventures between business and education will be required to construct the learning systems and software of the future. There is no precedent for the heavy front-end investment by educational institutions in state-of-the-art mediated learning systems.
- The mainstream higher education leadership is *not* responding to the opportunity within these challenges. Low morale, depression and a mood of hopelessness is spreading across

American higher education as the demographic dip of the traditional market takes hold. Instead of organizing to meet the expanding lifelong learning needs of the citizenry, the strategy of choice to meet the crisis is retrenchment of faculty and staff. The assumptions of the current educational model go largely unexamined. Many lifelong learning leaders are frustrated by this failure of leadership.

Updating the Model

The present educational model is now a century old. We tend to behave as though it is God-given and eternal. Yet even a cursory examination of the history of education reveals that a society's learning process is dynamic and changes as the needs, challenges and aspirations of that society change. In retrospect, we know that the rapidly evolving mass industrial economy located in urban centers and its counterpart in scientific agriculture required a strengthening of the nation's learning process in the last quarter of the nineteenth century. The new educational inventions met the challenge and laid the foundation for a very successful century. *My central thesis is that the nation is again at such an economic and cultural watershed requiring a quantum leap in citizen understanding and competence.*

This conclusion came into focus as part of inter-institutional planning processes begun by Delaware Valley colleges and universities in 1976. We had to conclude that the demographics were masking the real problem—the obsolescence of the educational model—and set about constructing a better model, which is now in the early stages of implementation.

The strengthened model is rooted in a fundamental analysis of changing learning requirements and the process by which they are met. It is essential to move past the *explicit* learning curriculum, which focuses on the intellectual and vocational skills, and remind ourselves that there has always been an *implicit*, almost invisible, curriculum which facilitates our learning of the roles, values, attitudes, and other affective dimensions required for living. We tend to forget that courage, risk-taking, manners, maleness, femaleness and a thousand other personal characteristics are learned behaviors. Indeed, we need to remind ourselves that the success of the *explicit* curriculum is heavily dependent on the effectiveness of the *implicit* curriculum. The evidence is clear that the rapid cultural changes of the past century have diminished the traditional indoctrinations of family, community and religious institutions, while the newcomer institutions of the peer group, media and the workplace have risen to new authority in the learning process.

The analysis strongly suggests that we must move past our fixation on the formal education *institution* as the primary agency of learning and begin to see the lifelong learning process in *systems* terms. I have proposed the construction of the *human learning system* as a useful way of seeing the comprehensive lifelong learning process in wholistic terms. Clearly, our species has always required and had a human learning system; but, up to now, it has never been an explicit vehicle for policy and program development.

In the *human learning system* strategy now being developed and implemented in the Philadelphia area, we see three basic action imperatives leading to a strengthened *system:*

- *It is essential that the citizenry understand the expanded tasks and responsibilities of their own lifelong learning and development.* With the decline of traditional indoctrinations, there are new dimensions of freedom and choice in what one is to become. But unless the freedom is related to the economic and social challenges, as well as the personal, we risk remaining in an empty "me-ism." Education has paid little attention to the issue of learner-preparation to engage the tasks of lifelong learning. It needs to have the highest priority.
- *It is essential that all institutions in the human learning system understand the systemic context and make adjustments to support the expanded, explicit learning agenda.* Family, community, church, school, college, media, workplace, etc., all need to be strengthened in support of a "living and working smarter" national goal.
- *It is essential that all institutions in the system learn to work together at local, regional and national levels.* Just as we have learned to think of the economy and our political life in *systems* terms, so we must now begin to bring the *human learning system* into consciousness and explicit guidance.

At first blush, an attempt to update and strengthen a primary system of American society seems to be an insuperable task. Yet our experience at implementing the components of the strategy over the past four years leaves us optimistic. We find individuals hungry for a better understanding of how to engage their lives, and we find most of the institutions within the system humble in the face of current realities and open to new understandings and activities. In our experience, we find the corporate educators, as represented in the American Society for Training and Development (ASTD), furthest along in understanding the new educational imperatives. The religious community is not far behind; having lost much of their earlier authority, thoughtful church folk are eager to test out new ways. The formal educational institutions, both basic and higher, are currently mired in the management of decline, but the continuing educators, as represented in National University Continuing Education Association (NUCEA), and the cutting-edge educators Morris Keeton manages to bring together in the Council for the Advancement of Experiential Learning (CAEL), are quickly moving toward a strengthened model. Based on very little experience at the Philadelphia Navy Yard, it appears that military educators are moving toward a sophisticated human resource development strategy. The media find themselves in last place in understanding their role and power in the nation's human learning system, but some new vitality and understanding of this role is appearing in both the Corporation for Public Broadcasting (CPB) and the Public Broadcasting Service (PBS), representing the nation's public broadcasting stations. In short, there is a far greater readiness for the necessary institutional transformation than any of us would have thought possible even a few years ago.

Within the past year or so two major trends in support of the strategy have become apparent. First, the nation's business leaders have come to the realization that we will not accomplish the necessary economic transformation to the information, high technology age without a parallel strengthening of our human resources. These leaders do not as yet have a specific strategy, but they are actively looking for one. Second, an examination of this fall's election reveals that many thoughtful governors and other elected officials have identified the centrality of the human resource issue for the nation to get moving again. It is clear that the human resource issue will be center stage in the '84 election.

Therefore, I offer the conclusion that the conceptual base for strengthening the nation's educational model is available. There is a growing readiness on the part of the citizenry and the supportive institutions to make the necessary adjustments. The political and economic climate for the transformation is warming. Based on the pilot experiences in implementing the components in Philadelphia, and elsewhere, the required adjustments are feasible within the present institutional infra-structures. Even seventy senior faculty at my institution, Temple University, have accepted the analysis and strategy as valid, and are busy reinventing their University through a multi-faceted project, appropriately titled, *A New University for a New Century*. As I see it, the issue now is to devise means to accelerate the transformation. The coming together of the lifelong learning leaders at the Lifelong Learning Leaders Retreat provides an opportunity for the representatives of the key associations and related organizations to explore the issue and ways to provide leadership to the transformation. My hope and advocacy is that the leaders come to consensus that the transformation is necessary and they come together on the strategy and tactics to bring it about. Unless educators rise to the task, others will and American education will be in for serious criticism, if not replacement, by other institutions.

Some Thoughts About An Action Agenda

The nation's lifelong learning leaders come together after a long period of institutional and professional fragmentation. Is it possible to come to some shared understandings and agendas? As I have just argued, I believe that the coming together process is already under way and the organization of the retreat is just one more event in the process. The leadership of the Coalition of Adult Education Organizations (CAEO) has sought to provide a forum for the coming together in the past, but the climate has not been ripe until now. If our experience in Philadelphia is any guide, we must allow for the working out of the suspicion, distrust, institutional and professional egotism that is an inevitable consequence of the decades of fragmentation. Hence, common understandings about the challenges facing American society and the direction of solving the problems are pre-requisite to any effective action agenda.

My thoughts about an action agenda follow:

- **Institutional consciousness-raising:** All of the institutions in the *human learning system* need to understand the new realities and the new tasks confronting them. If every association attending the retreat undertook to disseminate a consensus view on the realities and tasks to their membership, we would take a giant step forward in developing some common understandings among institutions, including schools, colleges, business, media, etc.

- **Citizen consciousness-raising:** As outlined earlier, increased citizen understanding of the new tasks of explicit lifelong learning is essential. If all of the associations worked together on a national program of such consciousness-raising, the effort would be more cost-effective and get the job done quickly. Arlon Elser, Phil Nowlen and I have been discussing such an approach with Phil Donahue, and more recently the task has been discussed with Bill Cosby. Clearly, a media approach is envisioned.

- **Stimulating pilot projects:** If part of an effective change-process depends on a better idea, and then its dissemination, another part is the organization of pilot projects which test and refine the implementation of the idea. What we have done in Philadelphia amounts to the tip of the iceberg. There is much to be done and all entrepreneurs ought to be encouraged by the associations. Morris Keeton is distributing a think piece on the organization of a national system of learner services, and it could become an important retreat outcome.

- **Developing a post-'84 legislative agenda:** As the pre-retreat questionnaire revealed, there is great interest in working together on the legislative front. In the two years we have before the human resource issue comes to political center stage,

an analysis of existing and possible legislation to speed the system strengthening process ought to be made on an inter-associational basis.
- **Development of linkages and networks:** All major policy shifts require the support of other constituencies beyond those directly affected. If we are to plant a strengthened self-directed, lifelong learning strategy within the framework of the American human learning system, then we must gain the support of business, political, communications and civic groups beyond our own associational network. A planned process of outreach, persuasion and coalition building needs to be organized.
- **Invention of learning system/software development process:** Earlier, I referred to the urgent need to invent new organizational mechanisms among educational providers to guide the development of mediated learning systems and related software. There is only the vague beginning of such a process, and it is surrounded by excessive competition. An inter-institutional, inter-associational group needs to get to work on this problem before the provider community loses control of the process.
- **Continuing intellectual and application development:** The last time the nation embarked on a major new social policy was in the mid-60's through the array of Great Society programs. Although the zeal was high and resources ample, there was a failure to refine the policy and program. Don McNeil, then at Wisconsin, and I tried vainly to persuade the Great Society managers to invest in such refinement, but to no avail. As we get ready for the update of the educational model, it is essential that such refinement be provided for.

Conclusion

I have sought to provide a context for the Lifelong Learning Leaders Retreat. The context includes a rapidly changing economic, social and political environment leading to a once-in-a-century update of the American educational model. I argue for that update to take place within the framework of the society's *human learning system* with new tasks for the citizenry and adjusted supportive capabilities on the part of families, communities, churches, schools, colleges, media, the workplace, etc. I have summarized the experience a few of us have had in implementing the model, and point to the feasibility of the approach. Finally, I have outlined a first-stage action agenda for consideration by the lifelong learning leaders.

Synthesis Comments on Reck Niebuhr's Position Paper

Through his position paper, Reck Niebuhr extends a challenge to lifelong learning leaders to change the century old educational model and to make the "quantum leap" in citizen understanding and competence which is necessary for educational institutions to be timely and effective.

Through his illuminating charts, Reck illustrates in a dynamic fashion where our human learning systems have been in the past, and he recommends an "information age paradigm" which can guide us in our future planning.

Educational administrators who are traditional in their views will likely take issue or be threatened by the projected changes and realities which Reck projected for the future if an educational system is to be successful tomorrow. On the other hand, those within our ranks who are futurists, innovators and advocates of change will applaud Reck's direct approach and systematic rationale which he has presented in his attempt to change the establishment.

1) PRE-INDUSTRIAL PARADIGM

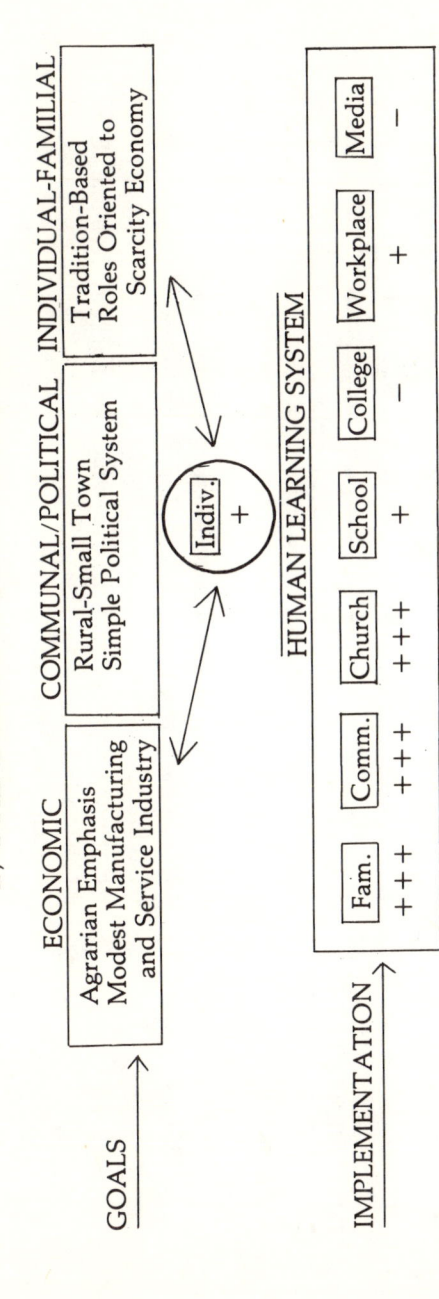

GOALS →

ECONOMIC	COMMUNAL/POLITICAL	INDIVIDUAL-FAMILIAL
Agrarian Emphasis Modest Manufacturing and Service Industry	Rural-Small Town Simple Political System	Tradition-Based Roles Oriented to Scarcity Economy

Indiv. +

HUMAN LEARNING SYSTEM

Fam.	Comm.	Church	School	College	Workplace	Media
+++	+++	+++	+	−	+	−

IMPLEMENTATION →

- High Indoctrination—Low Intentional Learning
- Traditional Institutional Domination
- Embedded System Management
- Formal Learning as Terminal Activity
- Curriculum Narrowly Defined
- System Inadequate to Changing Goals In Mid-19th Century

2) INDUSTRIAL PARADIGM

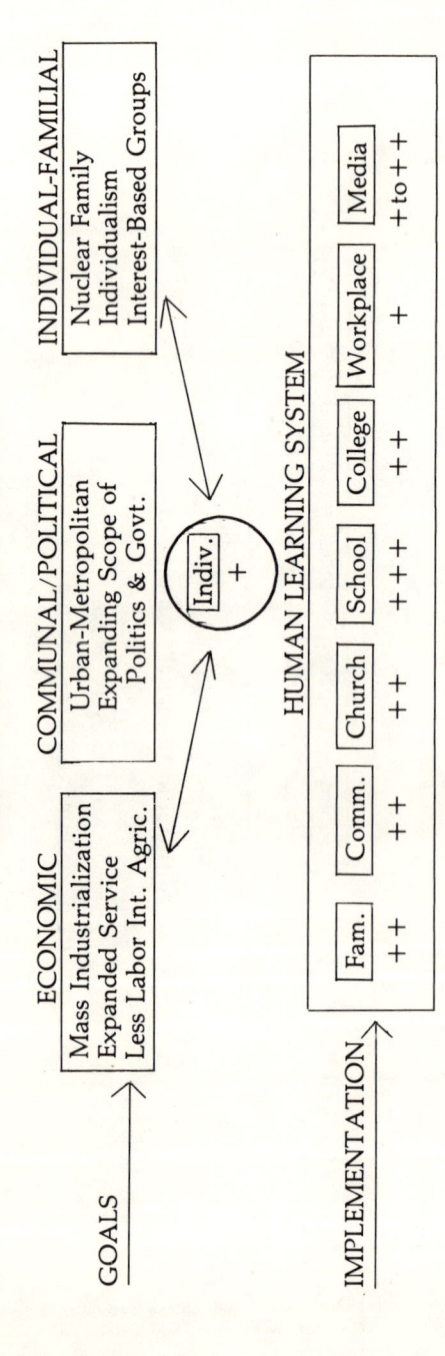

GOALS →

ECONOMIC	COMMUNAL/POLITICAL	INDIVIDUAL-FAMILIAL
Mass Industrialization Expanded Service Less Labor Int. Agric.	Urban-Metropolitan Expanding Scope of Politics & Govt.	Nuclear Family Individualism Interest-Based Groups

↕ Indiv. + ↕

HUMAN LEARNING SYSTEM

IMPLEMENTATION →

Fam.	Comm.	Church	School	College	Workplace	Media
++	++	++	+++	++	+	+ to ++

- Indoctrination in Social-Sexual-Religious Affairs
- Expanding Intentional Learning, Especially In Work Areas
- Declining "System Management"
- Expanded Role-Power of Formal Education But Still Terminal, Except for Extension
- System Successful for Century!
- Signs of Disarray Since '60s

3) INFORMATION AGE PARADIGM

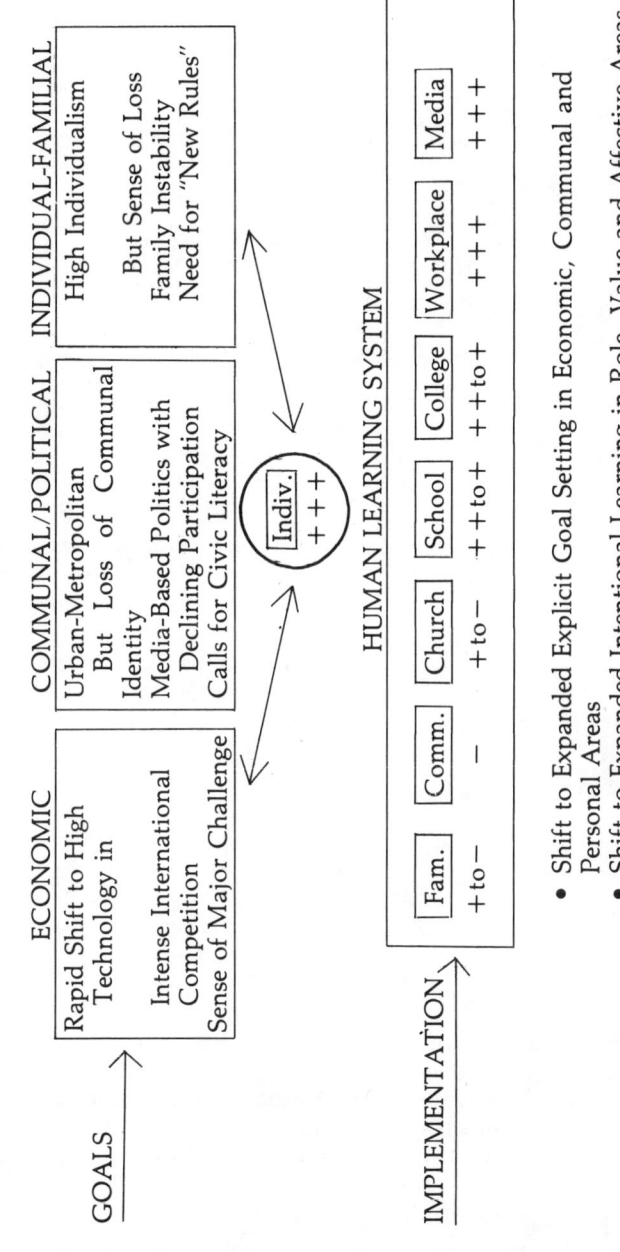

GOALS →

ECONOMIC
Rapid Shift to High Technology in
Intense International Competition
Sense of Major Challenge

COMMUNAL/POLITICAL
Urban-Metropolitan
But Loss of Communal Identity
Media-Based Politics with Declining Participation
Calls for Civic Literacy

INDIVIDUAL-FAMILIAL
High Individualism
But Sense of Loss
Family Instability
Need for "New Rules"

Indiv.
+++

HUMAN LEARNING SYSTEM

IMPLEMENTATION →

Fam.	Comm.	Church	School	College	Workplace	Media
+to−	−	+to−	++to+	++to+	+++	+++

- Shift to Expanded Explicit Goal Setting in Economic, Communal and Personal Areas
- Shift to Expanded Intentional Learning in Role, Value and Affective Areas
- Shift to Self-Directedness in Learning from Authority-Centered Pedagogy
- Shift to Lifelong Learning Commitment
- Shift to Explicit Learning System Guidance

Thurman White
NORMAN, OKLAHOMA

Dr. White has a distinguished career in higher education/continuing education administration. When serving as Vice President for Continuing Education at the University of Oklahoma, Dr. White was responsible for the development of the University's program which serves military bases throughout the world. He also was responsible for the development effort which led to the implementation of the University's Resident Continuing Education Center, which was supported initially by the W. K. Kellogg Foundation.

Thurman White has been active in professional association work, having served as President of both the National University Continuing Education Association and the Adult Education Association of the United States.

Dr. White currently serves as Vice Chancellor for Outreach for the Oklahoma Regents for Higher Education. In this capacity, he is responsible for the coordination of continuing education efforts of post-secondary education in Oklahoma.

A Loosely Coupled System For Adult Education Organizations

The principal proposition of this paper is that the common concerns of adult education organizations of America require a loosely coupled system of relationships. The proposition assumes two essential elements:
1. The adult education organizations of America are indeed tied together in purpose.
2. The totality of the adult education effort in America is, in fact, a social system.

Let us begin with the concept of "loose coupling." The phrase has been around a relatively short time, perhaps little more than a decade. An early and still useful explanation of the concept was presented by Karl E. Weick in the March, 1976, issue of the *Administrative Science Quarterly*. After noting that "loose coupling" connotes impermanence, dissolvability and tacitness as the crucial glue which holds the system together, Weick gives us seven potential functions of "loose coupling":

1. In a loosely coupled system, the related organizations are responsive to one another, but each preserves its own identity and separateness.
2. Loose coupling provides a unique sensitive sensing mechanism. The several organizations in a loosely coupled system preserve many independent sensing elements and therefore know, and are able to share, their environments better than is true for more tightly coupled systems which have fewer externally constrained, independent elements.
3. Loosely coupled systems facilitate localized adaptation of shared research findings, innovative programs and new technology. The localized adaptation is standardization.
4. Where the identity, uniqueness and separateness of the elements are preserved, the system potentially can retain a greater number of mutations and novel solutions than would be the case with a tightly coupled system. Loosely coupled systems may be elegant solutions to the problem that adaptation may preclude adaptability.

5. If there is a breakdown in one organization in a loosely coupled system, then this breakdown is sealed off and does not affect other parts of the system. While the decay of one organization is not critical to the effective functioning of the loosely coupled system, it also follows that it is difficult for the loosely coupled system to repair a defective element.
6. Since some of the most important elements in adult education organizations are teachers, classrooms, directors and institutions, it may be consequential that in a loosely coupled system there is more room available for self-determination by the actors. Discretion is more limited in a tightly coupled system but it does have the comfort of a clear channel for passing the buck.
7. A loosely coupled system holds the costs of administration and coordination to the absolute minimum. At the same time, the minimal amount of money required by the system carries the further consequence of less money as a means of affecting changes in the system.

The seven functions outlined by Weick are not only theoretically intriguing, they seem to fit a present need in the field of adult education. Before turning to an analysis of the "fit," it may be well to look at some of the disadvantages of the proposition. The first and perhaps most grievous disadvantage is the novelty of the concept—at least to the people in our field. We are much more comfortable in a discussion of organizational linkages when we have traditional and prototypal concepts under consideration. We are able, for example, to see how we might become "The American Council of Adult Education," or the "Congress of Adult Education Organizations," or the "American Federation of Adult Education," or the "Consortium," or the "Affiliated," or some other tried and true designation. We probably could not become known as "The Loosely Coupled System of American Adult Education." That very name would scare off the Daniel Boones and Alan Shepards in our midst. A more modest name, like "The Adult Education Secretariat for Inter-organizational Programs" would be just as descriptive and raise far fewer hackles. But the uncertainty of the untried and the unknown may be sufficient argument to foreclose a consideration of the concept by the leaders of some adult education organizations.

A second disadvantage of the proposition is its ambiguity. Is it really possible for organizations to retain their identity and function as integral parts of a system? Most of our experience has taught us that any time several organizations begin a formal relationship, the newly formed association begins to erode the identity and autonomy of the founding partners. In fact, the newly formed association frequently becomes competitive with the founders in the search for funds, prestige and program services. America is probably the foremost nation in all history to express its fierce commitment to personal independence by creating suffocating layers of bureaucratic templates. Given this penchant, the development of an abiding structure for a loosely coupled system may be beyond our ingenuity. The suggestion of a "Secretariat" will be examined later in this paper and may be an attractive approach to the problem of ambiguity.

A third disadvantage of the concept is its inherent dysfunctional elements. While the loosely coupled system permits easy adaptation and mutation at the local level, its loose permissiveness may actually encourage the practice of organizational espionage and thus thwart the diffusion of novel solutions to adult education problems. On the other hand, the system could produce by its improved sensing mechanism a superabundance of faddish responses and activities. The crucial factor is the selectivity with which the loosely coupled organizations share their concerns, resources, cooperative commitments and plans. In the abstract, the proposition is both functional and dysfunctional. It may perpetuate archaic tradition or it may diffuse innovative improvisation. Only in the structure of a loosely coupled system can we emphasize the functional potentials and overcome the dysfunctional.

We turn now to the notion that the adult education organizations may find that a loosely coupled system fits some of the current needs of the field. We will first examine six issues and concerns which are bigger than any one organization, some of which can only be approved with an understanding that everybody can do better than anybody. Next, we will examine the potential for linkages which may ease the pain of certain organizational sore spots.

The examination of issues and concerns writ large for the field is enormously simplified by an examination of the responses to the questionnaire sent to the retreat participants.

1. **Continued learning for professional adult education.** Houle's recent book, *Continuous Learning in the Professions* may have influenced many of the respondents, but whatever the reason, an overwhelming impression is the deep concern that runs throughout the organizations for more professionalism. Here are typical responses on this critical issue:
    a. teacher quality
    b. the image of the professional
    c. certification requirements, regulation and licensing
    d. keeping up with the state of the art
    e. a qualified and willing faculty
    f. effective and wide use of new technologies

2. **Access to learning.** As the population shifts to a median age of thirty plus, the significance of adult education is markedly enhanced. Most Americans have now assumed the responsibilities of maturity—they have jobs, families and public responsibility. They also are more critically vulnerable to the disabilities associated with ignorance and obsolescence. They want the educational delivery system to help them when and where it is possible for them to learn and to offer learning which is meaningful to them.

    The established delivery system is hopelessly lost as it tries to extend its effective pedagogy into an effective popagogy. *Both physical and cognitive access* are of crucial concern to the future of the entire field as seen by respondents who said:
    a. equal opportunity issues
    b. retraining for new careers
    c. computer literacy
    d. transition to high-technology jobs
    e. training of displaced workers
    f. training of homemakers

g. interstate delivery of programs
h. graying of America
i. completion rates
j. adaptation to variety of student clienteles
k. reaching individuals who need us most

3. **Resources.** Money for adult education is perceived by most practitioners as a finite and nonrenewable resource; so the scramble is to get all you can for your program. But the leaders who responded to the questionnaire are edging into the problem with a larger perspective. Perhaps the cooperative minds are psyching up to see possible ways of working toward an enlargement of the resource pool, cooperatively developed. Some quotes from the responses:
   a. adequate funding to continue operation
   b. tuition funding
   c. coordination of agencies which share the same source of major funding
   d. more effective use of resources
   e. enabling adult learners to pay for our services
   f. competition among providers of adult education
   g. marketing the services
   h. the ability to keep from being absorbed by others
   i. lack of a lobbying body
   j. influence of relicensing requirements on program budgets
   k. replacement of decreasing Federal support
   l. cost containment
   m. venture capital
   n. integrating resources

4. **Public appreciation.** The sense of this overarching concern is not for applause but the deeper meaning of appreciation as an informed favorable attitude. At heart, it is the need for a public philosophy which holds that the provision of lifelong learning is a public good. Such a public philosophy would find expression in the public responsibilities of educational boards, educational regents and trustees, congressmen, legislators, accrediting bodies, licensing boards, city councils,

county commissioners and other bodies politic. One gets a sense from the questionnaire responses that the public policy issues are too important to turn over to any one organization. Here are some examples:
a. turfdom
b. telecommunications
c. governmental influence on laws regarding training
d. government incentives for private sector involvement in adult education
e. governmental control of the quality of continuing education
f. perception of this Administration as anti-education
g. licensing requirements
h. conflicts between State and Federal policies
i. the "politicization" of national advisory councils
j. a national blueprint for adult education

In addition to the above common concerns reflected in the questionnaires, may I suggest three more:

1. **International and transnational.** Perhaps the root of all evil is not money as much as it is ignorance and obsolescence. On a global scale, this probably means that the people of America will best be served if their adult education leaders join with the adult education forces of the world to bring about educational equity. Indeed, the recent international assembly of adult educators in France may indicate that the opportunity is now ripe. It may also indicate that the market for adult education is international for some delivery systems, such as exchange seminar programs, and transnational for others, such as satellite courses.

2. **Research.** This concern is doubtless a part of the concern already noted for the professional development of the field. It is, however, of such import that isolating it will surely be seen as an appropriate emphasis. One can paraphrase an old axiom and say that a profession is known by the authors it keeps. Since adult education is a professional field, the concern for excellence in the advancement of the field through

unifying research and publication would appear to be a high priority shared by all the organizations.
3. **Future forecasting.** Change dominates our lives and our profession. Our organizations reflect it. Without forecasting, it is difficult to see a future in which we cope equitably with deceptive distractions and with compelling forces. With careful forecasting, it will be much easier to distinguish between the two, and to plan to educate for both. With a caveat to the inexactitude of the futurists, adult educators have too large a responsibility in an aging society to ignore the signals of change. We can only serve in a maximal way if we stay in touch with the massive demographic shifts; we can only be relevant if we stay in socio-economic context; we can only stay in business if we anticipate the emergence of new areas of ignorance and obsolescence.

Finally, we turn to an examination of a loosely coupled system as a means for inter-organizational linkages. Briefly, and at the risk of slightly misreading the data, the responses on collaborative efforts suggest that:

1. Several leaders, perhaps six, are ready to have joint meetings of key staff and officers.
2. Two or more leaders may be ready to share staff services, such as office space.
3. More than half the leaders see a need for collaboration on legislative relations.
4. As many as three, and perhaps more, leaders see the possibility of joint publication.
5. The co-sponsorship of research projects seems an agreeable possibility to several (at least four) leaders.
6. Co-sponsorship of regional and theme conferences appeal to six, and probably more, leaders.
7. Jointly conducted annual national conferences caught the enthusiasm of four leaders.
8. Publication exchanges have a green light from a half dozen leaders.

From the examination of the commonality of concerns among the leaders on critical issues and collaborative efforts, the concept of a loosely coupled system of relationships would seem to be a "best fit." The proposal of a Secretariat for inter-organizational programs would seem to be a modest mechanism for liaison purposes. The Secretariat is not an organization; it is conceived as simply a service office to be used as convenient by two or more organizations in a common effort. Many efforts may be ad hoc and short term; the relationship is concluded with amity. In the loosely coupled system there is no need to fight to maintain a project which has lived up to its expectations. Efforts are born, flourish and conclude. The coupling continues in succeeding efforts. An effort may have the participation of a dozen organizations, or half dozen or a brace. The Secretariat is to be available to any and all. Examples are many. Perhaps the following will be provocative:

1. A second galaxy conference. A dozen or more organizations as co-operators.
2. An international conference for adult educators by satellite —four organizations cooperating.
3. A program of internships for graduate students—two organizations cooperating.
4. A public information program to develop a public appreciation for lifelong learning—ten organizations cooperating.
5. A review of the futurists' scenarios for their adult education implications—eight organizations cooperating.
6. A conference on the public policy issues in State and Federal government—five organizations cooperating.
7. An agreement for group purchases of supplies, mailing services and insurance programs—seven organizations cooperating.

In summary, it is the position of this paper that a loosely coupled system is the concept which best fits the current needs for linkage among the adult education organizations in America. A simple structure for the implementation of the concept is a Secretariat for Inter-organizational Programs in Adult Education. Both the concept and the implementing Secretariat are targeted to the common concerns of all adult educators and are intended to facilitate the effective cooperation of adult education organizations in the pursuit of their common concerns.

**Synthesis Comments on
Thurman White's Position Paper**

At the opposite extreme from Michael Doyle's vision of a grand alliance is Thurman White's proposal for a loosely coupled system for adult education organizations. I find it the perfect complement to Doyle's sharply focused vision. Whether or not the Secretariat proposed by White is the instrument to enable loose coupling to occur, the image he creates is elegant and, I think, powerful. White encourages us to look for many ways to collaborate, large and small, short-burst and long-term, above-board and underground, loud and quiet, complicated and simple.

> . . . Many efforts may be ad hoc and short term; the relationship is concluded with amity. In the loosely coupled system there is no need to fight to maintain a project which has lived up to its expectations. Efforts are born, flourish and conclude. The coupling continues in succeeding efforts. An effort may have the participation of a dozen organizations, or half dozen or a brace. . . .

As one whose last book was based on the concept of "loose parts" as an approach to designing lifelong learning on both the personal and social levels, this has great appeal for me. I believe it provides an accessible place to start for virtually every person and organization represented in this conference. It would be disappointing if virtually everyone here did not leave this conference with the makings of at least one "loose coupling" in their pocket.

The following lists the results of the "practice" voting regarding Thurman White's position paper summary at the Tuesday, November 30, session.
1. How many are interested in having organizational committees on professional development explore common concerns? *90%*
2. How many are interested, on an access to learning basis, in having organizational equal opportunity committees meet to explore on common projects? *88%*
3. How many are interested in having the Federal relations committees of organizations meet regarding common projects? *100%*
4. How many are interested in having another CAEO Galaxy Conference? *70%*
5. How many are interested in having international relations committees of these organizations meet to discuss common projects? *62.5%*
6. How many are interested in having publications committee chairpersons come together to discuss common publications and research? *87%*
7. How many are interested in having meetings between Presidents and Executive Officers of associations meet to discuss future forecasting, such as we are doing here? *100%*
8. How many are interested in joint meetings of key staff and officers? *85%*
9. How many are interested in sharing staff services? *51%*
10. How many are interested in co-sponsorship of regional and theme conferences? *92%*
11. How many are interested in jointly conducting annual national conferences? *74%*
12. How many are interested in a publications exchange between associations? *100%*

IV. Issues Identification

The Issue Identification Process

The issues listed in this chapter were identified by the retreat participants in four concurrent meetings and were then voted upon by the entire body of retreat participants.

Electronic equipment was utilized to assess the collective importance of the issues which were initially identified by the participants. This same process was later utilized to ascertain the extent of group agreement concerning the recommendations which were made on alternatives which could lead to the resolution of issues.

The equipment which was utilized consisted of a voltage meter and a series of switches to which all retreat participants had access.

The analysis process was conducted under the following premises:
1. The entire data universe would be protected.
2. All items would be translated to similar semantical terms.
3. Any overlap or duplicative statements would be eliminated.
4. Each participant would vote on the statements they felt important to their association.

Under the above guidelines, it should be pointed out that items receiving a lower number of votes were not necessarily of lesser importance to every association represented. Ten associations, for example, could view an issue of primary importance and if the other ten associations did not see this issue as being encompassed in their associations' mission, and subsequently did not vote for it, the vote of record would be only fifty percent. On the other hand, the process did allow an assessment on the degree of total interest and the extent of collaborative resolution which could likely be expected.

By each issue on the following list, the percentage of total participant agreement is indicated.

Major Problems Confronting the Lifelong Learning Profession

		Balloting		
		1st	2nd	Tie
1.	Attitudinal barriers relative to vocational related retraining.	18%		
2.	Mistrust, communication problems and turf protection issues exist among adult education, business or community organizations.	38%		
3.	Continuing education has not moved into the formal structures of our American institutions.	31%		
4.	The public is unaware of available resources for adult learning.	45%	31%	
5.	It is unclear what the essential components and priorities for human resource development are.	34%		
6.	Lack of an effective model(s) for effective association collaboration (turf).	37%		
7.	Absence of a code of internal ethics to drive national strategy on human development.	16%		
8.	How do we assess lifelong learning needs/lack of a long-range implementation strategy(ies). e.g. capacity building/marketing—national/state/local.	40%		
9.	Failure of institutions to offer effective curricula that meets needs of lifelong learning students.	42%		

Issues Identification

		Balloting 1st	2nd	Tie
10.	Lack of awareness on part of general public, educational institutions, and teachers, on importance and need for adult and continuing education.	58%	59%	67%
11.	What should the role of lifelong learning be in improving the quality of life.	45%	32%	
12.	Failure to maximize the human resources in the development of human and technical productivity.	32%		
13.	How is basic literacy most effectively incorporated in the lifelong learning process/ineffective educational system that teaches: basic skills for youth and adults.	40%		
14.	Non-collaborative legislative efforts at all levels. How to affect/effect currently pending/future legislation relating to human resources development, training/adult education.	64%	78%	
15.	Lack of/what should be national/federal policy on lifelong learning.	64%	64%	
16.	Definition or conceptual framework for such terms as: human resources development, lifelong learning, community education, competency, high technology.	40%		
17.	How do we restructure and relocate our strategies to respond to future technologies.	52%	67%	

	Balloting		
	1st	2nd	Tie
18. How to carry out quality assessment and quality control in lifelong learning given its modes of delivery.	40%		
19. Unclear roles between the various providers and lack of agreement/cooperation.	32%		
20. How to organize for inter-association and inter-agency cooperation.	55%	59%	33%
21. How do we teach a whole new group of learners (in transition)/relates to deskilling of certain jobs.	26%		
22. Lack of articulation between institutions.	16%		

Mike Doyle explains the use of electronic balloting equipment (shown at far left). This equipment was used in plenary sessions to ascertain the degree of acceptance or level of priority which the total group gave to the recommendations which emminated from the small task groups' deliberations.

V. Issue Resolution Recommendations

The Process Utilized to Determine Alternatives to Major Issues

After determining the level of concern on each of the twenty-one issues, the retreat participants again divided into four concurrent settings to explore alternatives which could lead to the resolution of the four major issues which were identified. These issues were:

A. Collaborative effort among adult education associations and groups on legislative matters affecting them.
B. Increasing awareness of the importance of lifelong learning by the general public, educational institutions and teachers.
C. A national/federal policy on lifelong learning.
D. Restructure and reallocation of strategies to respond to future and emerging technologies.

The group facilitators each chose one of the four issues to discuss in their group, and were assigned the task of keeping notes on their group's recommendations.

Participants were allowed to participate in the discussion group which was dealing with an issue of major concern to their respective association and for which they had particular personal expertise. In an effort to further maximize the resource base represented at the retreat, the recommendation was made that there be no more than one representative per association in each discussion setting.

Approximately five hours were devoted to the concurrent small group identification and analysis of alternatives for issue resolution.

In a plenary session on the last day of the retreat, each facilitator reported his or her concurrent group's recommendations. Through the aid of the electronic balloting equipment, all participants then reacted to each of the recommendations which had been made.

Following are the recommendations which were developed on the four major issues by the four concurrent discussion groups. The percentages listed by each recommendation indicate the degree of support which all the retreat participants gave to each recommendation.

Ned Lester
BLACKSBURG, VIRGINIA

Early in his career, Dr. Lester served as Extension Agent in Bedford and Craig Counties in Virginia. He was also District Extension Agent prior to attending Florida State. In 1971, Dr. Lester became Associate Dean for Extension Field Service. Presently, he is serving as Associate Dean working in Administration and Operations for the Extension Division at Virginia Tech.

Dr. Lester is very active in professional and civic affairs. He has served on numerous AEA/USA committees and is presently serving as Chairman of the AAACE Development, Proposal and Consultation Committee.

Dr. Lester has received numerous honors and recognitions in his work. He is a co-author of a book and has written extensively in professional journals.

Report of the Recommendation-Development Group on
A. Collaborative Effort Among Adult Education Associations & Groups on Legislative Matters Affecting Them

>Ned Lester, Facilitator
>Paul Braden, NACCE
>Gary Eyre, AAACE
>Anthony Farma, USAES
>Henry Herzing, NATTS
>Morris Keeton, CAEL
>Reatha Clark King, COPA
>Dale Parnell, AACJC
>Tom Ridlehuber, AAACE
>Paul Tremper, NCEA

I. WHEREAS, the nation can anticipate:
   - increased international competition
   - critically limited resources
   - unacceptably high unemployment
   - heavy structural dislocation
   - unacceptably high rates of illiteracy, alcoholism and discouraged workers
   - uncoordinated and disjointed human resources legislation with no overall strategy,

   THEREFORE, IT IS RECOMMENDED:
   All the participating associations attending the retreat undertake a long-range collaborative effort to develop and implement a national lifelong learning development strategy. Also, that a proposal be designed (for funding) toward the development of a concept paper on a national policy pertaining to the development of lifelong learning. (Suggested lead agency AACJC, with all associations attending this retreat participating.) *100%*

II. WHEREAS, the lifelong learning movement lacks the necessary information exchange networks to support a meaningful collaborative support mechanism,

THEREFORE, IT IS RECOMMENDED:

A partial solution would be the Department of Commerce's productivity center resources should be made available to the adult learning associations. *86%*

III. WHEREAS, important legislation is now pending and action is needed by the participating organizations within the education community to address the needs and concerns of the adult learner. And,

Whereas the pending legislation will affect the productivity of the nation and will have impact on adult learners,

THEREFORE, IT IS RECOMMENDED:

A strategy be developed and a lead agency identified to respond to current legislation affecting adult education that is presently before Federal and State legislative bodies such as:

A. funding of eleven bills before Congress on education
B. legislative impact on post-secondary education
C. vocational and adult education consolidation effort
D. Pell grant
E. GI Bill—Volunteer Armed Forces
F. Partnership Training Act
G. Apple legislation
H. Department of Commerce Plans for 1990 census
I. Enterprise Zone program
J. Social Security legislation
K. Republican & Democrat party platform *92%*

IV. WHEREAS, a large number of adult education associations and organizations are not aware of legislative issues and matters as may be available through the American Council on Education efforts,

THEREFORE, IT IS RECOMMENDED:

AAACE be lead agency to meet with ACE to determine effective ways for those associations and organizations concerned with adult and continuing education can be better informed on legislative matters pertinent to their adult and continuing education interest. *66%*

V. WHEREAS, it is important that the participating organizations and their members be kept informed of the results and activities emerging from this conference,

THEREFORE, IT IS RECOMMENDED:

AAACE develop communications to participating associations on follow-up to all recommendations emerging from this conference, and each association report to its members the results of the conference. *95%*

In plenary sessions, the small group reports were presented and voted upon by all participants. Here, Mary Grefe is shown presenting recommendations which were made by one of the small task groups.

Mary Grefe
DES MOINES, IOWA

Mary Grefe is President of Lead Associates, Ltd., a firm specializing in improving the quality of leadership, both individual and in organizations. In this capacity, she has traveled widely, conducting workshops or keynoting conventions, and has been interviewed numerous times on television and radio.

In 1979-1981, Mary Grefe was the National President of the American Association of University Women (AAUW).

Mrs. Grefe enjoys a national and international reputation as an adult educator and spokesperson for women's issues. She has served on delegations in Copenhagen, Japan, Scotland and Canada.

She is a Past-President of the National Adult Education Advisory Council, and in 1972 she represented President Nixon as his personal representative to the UNESCO World Conference on Adult Education in Tokyo, Japan. She is listed in "Who's Who in the International Community."

Report of the Recommendation-Development Group on
B. Increasing Awareness of the Importance of Lifelong Learning by the General Public, Educational Institutions and Teachers

> Mary Grefe, Facilitator
> Harry Allen, NCEA
> Lowell Eklund, NACCE
> Sharon Faison, USAES
> Quentin Gessner, NUCEA
> Andrew Hansen, ALA
> Jerry Miller, ACE
> Linda Resnik, PBS
> Rawlein Soberano, NACAE

I. WHEREAS, the general public should be aware of and understand:
- the importance of continuing to learn; learning never ends
- the need to develop a willingness to learn
- learn how to learn
- the most efficient and economical ways to learn
- what resources are available to help

THEREFORE, IT IS RECOMMENDED:

1. One day out of American Education Week be designated Lifelong Learning Day, with all of the associations represented at this retreat and others not present being co-sponsors. *88%*
2. A professional public information campaign should be conducted to alert the nation's working press to the field's importance, achievements, problems and needs. As a part of this campaign, nationally syndicated features and columns should be placed in both print and nonprint media. *86%*
3. A lifelong learning hotline should be established for individuals and professionals as a referral center for basic information. This could be financed by providers of lifelong learning paying a fee. *58%*

4. Policy-makers and opinion-leaders outside the field of education should be targeted for improved communications. *91%*
5. A national speakers' bureau should be established to encourage wider use of the best speakers from the lifelong learning field by other organizations outside the field or at their annual meetings. Each of the associations represented here should make such a list available, and should also utilize the list as resources for their meetings. *75%*
6. To implement the professional public information campaign, the development of a steering committee to develop a process and seek funding. *92%*

II. WHEREAS, the traditional educational providers of lifelong learning should be aware of: (This relates to higher education, rather than K–12.)
- educational institutions are only one among many providers; they no longer have a monopoly.
- the importance of a college degree is declining. The marketplace is becoming the determining factor as to whether students go to college.
- the majority of college students are over 25 and are part-time students.
- Frequently, the personnel resources for providing opportunities for adult learning are not available, because the faculty is out working for the private sector.
- Traditional educational systems are in danger of becoming obsolete and out of "sync" with the needs of society.

THEREFORE, IT IS RECOMMENDED:
That the American Council on Education should take a leadership role in making the leadership and governing boards of post-secondary institutions aware of the growth, character, needs and promise of the lifelong learning area. *89%*

III. WHEREAS, the role of other providers of lifelong learning should be:
- the need to make more people aware of resources from such providers as libraries.

- that the media can play a supporting role and enhance the concept of lifelong learning as well as be a provider.
- that business and industry need to be aware of the maximum benefits of collaboration and make maximum use of educational institutions in the providing of lifelong learning opportunities.

THEREFORE, IT IS RECOMMENDED:

1. The lifelong learning hotline recommended previously should be very helpful in making people aware of providers in addition to the traditional educational institutions. *52%*
2. All of the organizations represented here continue to utilize the media as a provider, and involve them in the promotion of lifelong learning, locally and nationally. *88%*
3. That the local affiliates of the organizations represented here be encouraged to replicate this conference at the local level. *66%*
4. That ASTD use its contacts with the human resource development leaders in business and industry to work toward effective collaboration with the educational institutions in providing lifelong learning. *88%*

Roger Hiemstra
FAYETTEVILLE, NEW YORK

Dr. Hiemstra is currently Professor and Program Leader, Adult Studies, at Syracuse University. This position involves research in adult education, teaching adult education graduate courses, advising graduate students and coordinating the adult education program.

Dr. Hiemstra has also served as a faculty member in adult education at Iowa State University, the University of Nebraska, Wayne State University, and the University of Michigan. Additionally, he has been a Mott Administrative Intern in Community Education and a County Extension Agent.

Dr. Hiemstra has published extensively, having authored three books and numerous articles on adult and continuing education. He currently serves as Editor of *Lifelong Learning—The Adult Years*, and is Chairman of the Commission of Professors of Adult Education.

Report of the Recommendation-Development Group on
C. A National/Federal Policy on Lifelong Learning

Roger Hiemstra, Facilitator

William Barton, ACHE
Harold McAninch, AACJC
Joe Mills, AVA
Fran Spinelli, CAEO
Gene Whaples, AAACE
Ken Young, NUCEA

PREAMBLE AND POLICY STATEMENT

In the United States, there exists a rich history and heritage of self-reliance, individual responsibility, risk-taking, voluntary group action and creative problem-solving by citizens. Most such qualities have been embodied within a framework of political democracy and free enterprise. However, in recent times, these qualities and the value structures that undergird them have not been embraced by all citizens either because of feelings of alienation, or because the equal distribution of resources has not been possible.

The past few years have seen the American society faced with such issues as rapid technological change, the relocation of industry with concurrent employment changes, a constant influx of new populations, changes in family structures and many new or evolving cultural attitudes. All such changes, and many more that could be listed, have created a plaguing need for many citizens to reconcile traditional values and beliefs.

Such a need has resulted in a situation not unlike that faced some 100 years ago, when the United States was beginning the move from an agragrian society to an industrial one. The displacements, changes and new values required then have parallels now:
- millions are currently unemployed or underemployed
- millions of people are illiterate or under-educated
- millions are below poverty levels

Many more examples related to crime, divorce, suicide, drug abuse, etc., could be given to dramatize the crisis situation in which this country currently finds itself.

THEREFORE, the people of this country commit themselves to a national policy promoting the development of human resources through the continual education, training, and re-training of United States residents. The intent of this policy is to help each individual, family unit and community reach its potential, so that this country can maintain its leadership role among nations of the world. *97%*

RECOMMENDATIONS:
1. Disseminate the policy statement to selected Federal officials and seek its inclusion in the President's 1983 State of the Union message. *94%*
2. Disseminate the policy statement to officials of both the Democratic and Republican parties and seek its inclusion in their national platforms. *97%*
3. Disseminate the policy statement to all appropriate national advisory councils and seek their formal endorsement. *99%*
4. Disseminate the policy statement to officials of all groups represented at this retreat, and seek their formal endorsement. *97%*
5. Identify other groups, associations and agencies (both public and private) potentially interested in the policy statement, such as the Business Roundtable, National Chamber of Commerce, National Council/Associations of State Directors, etc., and seek their formal endorsement. *99%*
6. Disseminate the policy statement to the Domestic Policy Association and solicit their study, endorsement and implementation ideas. *81%*
7. Disseminate the policy statement to all local, regional and state organizations or networks affiliated with groups represented at this retreat, and seek their formal endorsements. The intent of this recommendation is to begin to impact legislation, programs and action at the local level on up so that a national policy can be implemented from the bottom up, rather than top down. *88%*
8. Ask each group represented at this retreat to assign one person as a representative to future meetings needed for further developing and implementing strategies related to this policy. *94%*

9. Seek further support from the major foundations and/or other support groups to enhance the dissemination, endorsement and strategy implementation through a national meeting of at least a hundred professional and consumer groups. *90%*
10. Seek further support from major foundations and/or other support groups to establish a secretariat that will be charged with further enhancement and development of the policy. *78%*
11. Design an affidavit for personal affirmation of the policy statement to be disseminated through organizations that reach the masses, such as county extension offices, vocational-technical schools, etc. The affidavits would be funnelled back to the secretariat group and other groups for uses deemed appropriate. *61%*

Issues and alternatives for their resolution were identified in concurrent small group meetings. Roger Hiemstra is shown here in his role as facilitator/recorder in one of the small group settings.

Everette Nance
ST. LOUIS, MISSOURI

Dr. Everette Nance currently serves as Associate Professor of Education Administration and Director of the Midwest Community Education Development Center at the University of Missouri-St. Louis. Dr. Nance's previous experience includes serving on the faculties of Ball State University, Western Michigan University and Central Michigan University. Additionally, he has been a YWCA Program Director.

Dr. Nance has published extensively in the area of community education, and has served in a variety of leadership roles with professional associations. Currently, he is a member of the Board of Directors of the National Community Education Association.

Grants activities and fund-raising are also specialties of Dr. Nance. During the past ten years, he has directed grants awarded from eight foundations and departments of government, totalling approximately two million dollars.

Report of the Recommendation-Development Group on
D. Restructure and Reallocation of Strategies to Respond to Future and Emerging Technologies

>Everette Nance, Facilitator
>
>Dee Brock, PBS
>William Fowler, NHSC
>Anne Marie McCartan, AAHE
>Richard Millard, CoPA
>Edward Scannell, ASTD
>Carol Stoel, FIPSE
>Elizabeth Stone, ALA
>Rick Ventura, NACAE

Basic Strategies: We need to determine how our institutions need to modify or change their structures so that they can use developing technologies more effectively with potential learners.

To accomplish the above, associations and institutions must take into consideration:
1. The kinds of "new" technologies which are already affecting their capacity to deliver services, and
2. The demographics of a changing society (e.g. obsolete jobs, changing workforce, third world production, minorities and women).

Goals: In order to address the above issue, the group decided to focus on future needs. Therefore, a futuristic process was utilized in goal determination. Goals were developed in the two following areas:
   A. The consideration of institutional and association responsiveness as they relate to the needs of the learner, and
   B. The structural changes which institutions need to consider if they are to be able to respond to emerging technologies.

A. LEARNER RELATED GOALS
1. To develop a population that is able to cope with and have skills to deal with new technologies.

2. To make various populations aware of the scope of educational alternatives which are available to them and to change their attitudes regarding learning as an ongoing process.
3. To assure that learning opportunities will be available at the time and place to meet learner needs.
4. To promote the idea that "education" should be integrated into life experiences, and that knowledge and skills obtained through the educative process is transferable.

STRATEGIES FOR LEARNER GOALS
- 1a. develop "user-friendly" technologies
- b. begin exposing learners to new technologies early on in their education and more effective continuity in the sequence of programs throughout formal education. How? Through better articulation by institutions, and by adult education organizations:
  1. supporting legislation
  2. working with their clients in helping them articulate better
  3. supporting demonstration projects
  4. investigating and understanding how new technologies can be accessible and teachable to all types of populations.
- 2–4a. demonstrate benefits of lifelong learning
  - b. clarify the scope of "learning" and market it that way. (Help people do life planning.)
  - c. put vocational and technical training in broader context through curriculum development, teacher training and similar efforts in the workplace
  - d. learn more about learning

B. STRUCTURAL GOALS
  1. To promote closer integration between those designing educational systems and packages, and those institutions and individuals who will take advantage of new technologies.
  2. To promote institutional flexibility in responding to emerging technologies considering the following:
     a. continuous internal and external assessment

b. faculty or trainer development
   c. fiscal resources needed
   d. physical resources needed
   e. administrative resources needed
   f. collaborative efforts with other organizations and institutions

STRATEGIES FOR STRUCTURAL GOALS

1. By the year 2000, a closer relationship should exist between the producers and designers of educational systems and the potential learner.
   Educational institutions could:

   "Court" one or two companies within an industry (e.g. computer, television) and work with them on projects to design usable applications of their products. One part of this partnership would be making the public aware of what has occurred.

   Do academic planning which is adaptable to needs of hardware/software producers.

   Bring together producers with learners to develop better products.

   Provide inventory or clearinghouse on what is being produced and is available, or act as "brokers" for learners to make them aware of all types of technology and settings available for their benefit.

2. By the year 2000, we need to have built flexibility into institutional planning. Inherent in this is a capacity of continuous assessment related to inter-intra-extra organizational goals and objectives as they impact upon the learner.
   a. Flexible finance formulas and support.
   b. Institutions should include public and private institutions in helping finance all types of learning, i.e., investigate areas of support outside traditional governmental sources of funding.
   c. Develop a public policy on lifelong learning and support of human resource development. This is particularly important at the state level.

THEREFORE, IT IS RECOMMENDED:
1. That the associations collaborate on a function and process of being a "clearinghouse" for efforts between producers and users of new technologies. *75%*
   a. Begin by finding out current and projected efforts by each association.
   b. Broaden that by gathering and sharing information on efforts going on between producers and educational institutions, business, community agencies, etc.
   c. Having gathered this information, associations can then work together on various efforts, or specific associations can become primary sources of information on various technologies and share this expertise with the others.
2. The issue of funding formulas and their relation to funding for these enterprises can be investigated by the National Association of College and University Business Officers (NACUBO), CASE and the State Higher Education Executive Officers (SHEEO). *65%*
3. Establish a task force including representatives of secondary and post-secondary education associations to better understand the impact of the new technology on the learner and improve continuity for students. This group could develop an agenda for making a case to State and Federal officials. *65%*
4. Every association represented here, and others not present, should look at the demographic and workplace projections of the future and review these in light of their service populations. Every association should work to change basic attitudes to incorporate the concept of learning as an integral part of life experiences. *75%*
5. Initiate demonstration projects and share information on these projects with the technology clearinghouse. *56%*

The Airlie Retreat Center is located in the Virginia countryside on the foothills of the Blue Ridge Mountains.

Ronald Gross
GREAT NECK, NEW YORK

Ronald Gross is director of The Independent Scholarship Project, sponsored by the Fund for the Improvement of Postsecondary Education (U.S. Department of Education). He is also Senior Consultant to the College Board's Office of Adult Learning Services, President of Writers in the Public Interest; Adjunct Associate Professor of Social Thought at New York University, and a member of the University Seminar (Columbia) on Higher Education.

Long active in the fields of education and social change, Gross has published a dozen books. Among the most recent is *The Lifelong Learner* (Simon and Schuster), commended by critics including Ivan Illich, Alvin Toffler, Isaac Asimov, Caroline Bird, Nat Hentoff, and John Holt, and endorsed by leading educators such as Clark Kerr, Malcolm Knowles, Rosalind Loring, J.R. Kidd and Neil Postman. *The New York Times* profiled him as the founder of "The Invisible University."

Gross' other investigations and writings in lifelong learning have been sponsored and published by such agencies as the National Institute of Education, the U.S. Office of Education, the New York State Education Department, Phi Delta Kappa, the National Endowment on the Arts, and the Federal Interagency Committee on Education. Each year since 1977, Gross has written the official interpretive report of the annual National Conference on Adult Education, published in *Lifelong Learning*, the journal of the Adult Education Association of the U.S.A.

In 1976, Gross was commissioned to write the official American Education Bicentennial Essay on Lifelong Learning, "A Nation of Learners," which became the title contribution to the Office of Education's Bicentennial volume.

VI. Synthesis

Success in Accomplishing Conference Goals

The first thing I'd like to say is that, speaking merely as one participant, I personally feel that we have, together, succeeded handsomely in achieving the four goals which Wendell Smith posed for this conference at our opening session.

There is ample evidence that we have become not only *better acquainted*, but in various ways intrigued, impressed and empathetic with one another. Nothing could be clearer than that we have witnessed not only those "loose couplings" of Thurman White's, but that we've also seen the burgeoning of, additionally, lively liaisons, incipient alliances, nascent partnerships and, to put it plainly, mutually advantageous deals.

Secondly, we have certainly identified—with the inspiration of the superb papers by Lloyd Davis, Michael Doyle, Herman Niebuhr and Thurman White—and with the additional assistance of Mike's marvelous voting mechanism (surely the most notable addition to the American electoral process since Richard Daley stole the Chicago vote for Jack Kennedy), the *key issues* likely to confront lifelong learners and lifelong learning associations during the next decade.

Third, through the resourceful services of our facilitators—Mary Grefe, Everette Nance, Roger Hiemstra and Ned Lester—we have carefully considered both individual and collective *alternatives* to address and resolve those issues.

And, finally, we have formulated strong, clear, actionable *recommendations* for ourselves and others.

I congratulate you on this fine performance.

Lifelong Learning is Perennial

We have talked much of the *contemporary* imperative for lifelong learning in America in these mid-80's. I agree that we do need to define, for ourselves and others, what makes what we do fit the temper of the times in a compelling way.

But I'd like, too, to keep in mind that what we are doing is *perennial*. The importance and beauty of our work is that it speaks directly to a basic need of all humans, in all times and places.

Reck Niebuhr's illuminating charts on how the human learning system has changed and is changing are most useful—but I'd also stress that the more it changes, the more it remains the same. Our work addresses something deeper in human nature than the technological, demographic and cultural crisis we are undergoing today.

What we do speaks to something basic in human nature: Our destiny is learning, knowledge, understanding, and what we do speaks to something basic in the *American* spirit. The "pursuit of happiness" must mean the highest happiness, the happiness of the good life, clearly seen, prudently pursued through the cultivation of our capacities.

America has always been a nation of learners.

The Value of Our Work

Why are we here? To me, the answer is simple, but compelling. We are here because we believe that it is *people* that matter most, and we want to have a hand in helping them to become everything they are capable of being—or, at the least, to become more than they are, and often more than they thought possible. Your members' offerings—whether they are courses or programs, conferences or institutes, community services or nontraditional college degrees, career planning or remedial work—are, all of them, *levers for life-change*.

We are strengthening the healthiest, most life-affirming impulses in the people of our communities. Together, we are involved in some of the most constructive work going on in this country today. We work with the only truly inexhaustable resource left, and also the most fragile: the spirit within each human being to shape and reshape the self, in ways large and small, to become more fully what only he or she was born to be.

Pursuing that goal, you are not only making your associations work, you are playing a role in making the American dream work as well.

In this shared adventure, I believe we can find work worthy of the best that is in us, in our associations, in their members and in the learners we serve.

The New Improving American: Nancy Ignazio Africano

One of the first things we agreed upon at this conference was that we wanted to keep the lifelong *learner* himself—or herself—squarely in view as the target and the beneficiary of all our associational and institutional activity. I couldn't agree more with this commitment. My chief concern and enthusiasm over the past five years has been to listen as closely and as sensitively as I could to what lifelong learners of all kinds are trying to tell us about their needs, their aspirations, their problems, their hopes. In fact, when people ask me just what exactly I do in my various roles and functions in this field, I explain it by saying that I listen as hard as I can to learners themselves, and then I work as hard as I can to articulate what I hear to others who want to hear.

So both from your point of view and mine, I think a fitting way to reflect on the issues and problems and proposed solutions which have constituted our agenda is now to bring it down to the individual learner. I was started thinking about this by something Thurman White said in presenting his paper. He wondered out loud about how wonderful it would be if all the missions of the associations represented here were actually fulfilled. What if the goals and aspirations of our public school adult education programs, our media-based instructional offerings, our colleges and universities, our nontraditional degree programs, our human resources development efforts—what if all these and others actually could accomplish what they seek?

What a transformation that would make the lives of Americans, Thurman suggested.

Well, let's play with that for a moment.

When I did, I found myself thinking about a single person and what such a learning society might mean to him or her. At first, I thought about it generically, calling my imaginary person the New Improving American. But then I began to see the figure more clearly, and a definite, if composite, person took shape in my mind. While the *composite* is imaginary, everything this person *says* and everything that *happens* to her, has been said to me by the learners I've interviewed in writing my last two books. All I've done is to put together the pieces the way they might fall together for millions of real people, if Thurman's vision could be realized—if the people and institutions and organizations you represent were enabled to do what you pledged yourselves to do.

I call my New Improving American by a portmanteau name indicative of the kind of mix which will characterize our emerging American population. Her name is Nancy Ignazio Africano, and she is 1/3 Hispanic, 1/3 Black and, of course, all American.

Nancy is a single parent of 1.1 children. When Nancy thinks back over her life, she sees it as permeated with, and punctuated by, things she's learned that have impelled her in new directions, made her aware of a new dimension of herself, given her new skills, led her into new experiences. She will tell you that "I like to always be involved in learning something new, whether it's in connection with my job, my children, or just for myself. I know there are certain things that I *must* learn at certain times in my life," she says. "But I've always also known that there are things I just plain *want* to know, for my *soul's* sake. Both are important to me. Both have helped to make me what I am."

Nancy's adult education as an American began in Los Angeles soon after she arrived from El Salvidor. She learned English as a second language, as well as taking adult basic education courses, at the Watts Learning Center, part of the LA Unified School District. She still has in her closet, as one of her proudest possessions, the jacket which the Watts Center conferred on her along with her certificate, with the insignia of the Center on the back.

But that was many years ago. Nancy's learning has taken her a long way since then. She moved to Chicago from Los Angeles, where she recalls continuing her learning not at a school, but through her local public library. She found that by taking courses at the library, largely on the weekends when she had the most time, and using the videocassettes provided by the Study Unlimited Project sponsored by the Chicago Public Libraries and the City Colleges of Chicago, she could pursue her first two years of college at her own pace. "I was a little afraid of a college classroom," she confesses. "At the library, I could go at my own pace. If it was above my head I could just listen again, and no one would know."

It was in this period that Nancy also took two correspondence courses, one in accounting, the other in Latin American Poetry.

Nancy moved to Brooklyn, New York, around this time, and was gratified to learn about Empire State College, through which she could work toward her B.A. in Business Administration without attending classes. The Regents Credit Bank and Empire State's policy on awarding credit for experiential learning gave her quite a start, so that it only took a year and a half for her to finish her degree. "It was hard work all the way," she remembers. "But my employer was wonderful about encouraging me and helping me shape some work in the office to satisfy some of the requirements. He believed that every person, like every company, should be devoting 10 or 15 percent of their resources to research and development, to create new capacities and products, and that for a *person*, that means developing new skills and deeper understanding."

Such an employer, as you might well imagine, saw Nancy as a promising candidate for his management development program, which he was using to create a new cadre of executives by drawing from the underutilized talent pool among women and minorities. "Why compete with every other firm for those Harvard MBAs," he had told his Personnel Vice President, "when we can get topflight talent and train them, through our arrangement with N.Y.U., to be every bit as good as we need."

That was twenty years ago. Today, on this first day of December, 1982, Nancy is winding up her affairs at the corporation. After having served by special dispensation of the Board for two years beyond the usual retirement age of 65, she will step down as Chief Executive Officer of the corporation at the end of this year.

Moreover, Nancy's continuing education, which has gone on as intensively as ever, has once again impelled her in a new direction. Her adult education has consisted recently of annual participation in the Aspen Institute's Executive Program, and that opportunity to reconsider basic issues of our society has given her a fresh impulse not only to learn, but to begin to teach others. "I've joined Ken Boulding's Academy of Independent Scholars," she said in a recent interview about her retirement plans. "I want to devote the next fifteen years to studying and writing about the role of learning in facilitating life transitions and making it possible for each of us to become all that we are capable of being."

At the end of each day, the retreat participants spent time in the registration/lounge area informally continuing discussions. (Top) Reck Niebuhr and Everette Nance; (bottom) Mary Grefe, Harry Allen, and Gene Whaples.

VII. Sponsors

W. K. Kellogg Foundation

W. K. Kellogg's intention was clear at the outset when he established the philanthropic organization in 1930 which bears his name. His Foundation would "help people to help themselves." The man who pioneered the ready-to-eat breakfast cereal company in 1906 never wavered from his ideals during the years until his death in 1951 at the age of 91. He said, "I'll invest my money in people," adding apologetically: "It has been much easier to make money than to spend it wisely." History vouches that Mr. Kellogg was successful in each endeavor.

Recognizing society's difficulty in putting available knowledge to use for human benefit, Mr. Kellogg gave to this Foundation its distinctive commitment, "for the application of knowledge to the problems of people." The Foundation remains true to this philosophical concept and addresses significant human issues with direct, pragmatic answers.

From modest beginnings, with programs relating to the health and educational needs of children in south central Michigan, the Foundation has grown to a position of national and international prominence for its assistance in meeting social goals. It is numbered among the largest philanthropic organizations in the United States, distributing more than $585 million in grants during its five decades. As a private grant-making Foundation, it provides financial assistance to organizations and institutions that have identified and analyzed problems and have designed constructive action programs aimed at practical solutions. It currently assists projects on four continents including the United States and Canada, Latin America, Australia, and selected European countries.

Human needs outweigh the resources of all private philanthropies. But the role of private dollars in meeting social goals often is critical and catalytic. The analysis of the social benefit of philanthropic supported activities in furthering the human condition provides convincing evidence of the wisdom of pluralism—public and private—in serving mankind.

Kellogg Foundation Programming for the 1980s

At the program implementation level, the Foundation is committed to improving educational opportunities that prepare individuals for work and citizenship and to improving services which benefit people. In some instances the approaches must also include defining public policy where it is inadequately stated or ineffectual in meeting its responsibility for the public's well being.

Toward those aims, five areas of major concentration are identified for programming in the coming years. First, there is a dedication to expand opportunities for adult continuing education. The next three key issues are linked under a commitment to improve human well being. They are, activities to promote health and prevent disease; design and implement coordinated cost-effective health services; and, strengthen productive agriculture. The fifth concern is to foster leadership capacity among individuals, primarily in the fields of agriculture, education, and health.

Expanding Opportunities for Adult Continuing Education

Education, in many forms and circumstances, is society's best hope for stimulating and bringing about the changes that improve the quality of human life. And yet, adults who attempt to continue their education and training generally find a frustrating absence of any coherent, coordinated learning system to meet their purposes. Professionals of all kinds represent a distinct segment of learners who also need to update their education as new knowledge is created and to expand their understanding of the implications of new developments within their field. But, here again, there is lack of clarity in the purposes and patterns of lifelong and continuing professional education.

Therefore, a goal of the Kellogg Foundation is to improve adult continuing education beyond the initial phase of general and occupational education and training. That initial phase in the typical pattern of formal instruction is where matters have traditionally started and stopped within institutions. We are encouraging new directions for programs which prepare adults for improved performance in their work and broaden their understanding of personal goals and opportunities in their lives.

Gary Eyre
WASHINGTON, D.C.

Gary Eyre is Executive Director of the newly formed American Association for Adult and Continuing Education. His previous experience includes serving as Executive Director of the Presidentially appointed National Advisory Council on Adult Education, where he was responsible for providing leadership in the development of policy, program direction and project thrusts in the area of adult education.

Dr. Eyre has received numerous awards and honors, including several from the two associations which recently merged to form AAACE, the Adult Education Association of the U.S.A. and the National Association for Public Continuing and Adult Education.

The American Association for Adult and Continuing Education

Project One of AAACE

On July 29, 1981, the AEA/USA Development Committee and Dr. Wendell L. Smith submitted a proposal to the W. K. Kellogg Foundation, and sixteen months later on November 29, 1982, the Lifelong Learning Leaders Retreat held its opening session in the wooded countryside of Virginia. Far removed from busy offices and urban distractions, the conference site of Airlie House provided the participants with an atmosphere that was conducive to addressing the issues and identifying the thrusts confronting the adult and continuing education area of lifelong learning. The leaders goal for the retreat—to determine the ways in which professional associations could most effectively provide their members with the direction and service needed to bring about collaborative efforts—was realized.

During the multiple planning stages for the conference, the original sponsor organization, the Adult Education Association of the U.S.A., was engaged in a monumental organizational consolidation plan with the National Association for Public Continuing and Adult Education (NAPCAE). Just two weeks prior to the Leaders Retreat, the combined membership of AEA and NAPCAE finalized this consolidation effort at the National Adult Education Conference in San Antonio, Texas. The merger resulted in the chartering of the American Association for Adult and Continuing Education (AAACE).

Hosting the Lifelong Learning Leaders Retreat was the first major project for the new association, AAACE. Thanks to Ms. Beverly Copeland, Associate Executive Director, and Mrs. Donna M. Gruntz, Director of Membership Services, together with the headquarters' support staff, the Retreat far exceeded expectations.

AAACE was honored to host the retreat and facilitate the trend-setting innovations that developed. These innovations went beyond cooperative partnerships to the common concern of the associations—the well-being of the adult client as a learner. The physical environment, the staff support, and association leadership all assisted the conferees to look at logical extensions of the adult/continuing education trends, and to stretch a bit beyond verbal communication to thoughtful cooperation, a bit beyond alliances to a point where association distinctions vanish altogether. Acknowledging the fact that separate associations will always be at hand, the retreat participants did forecast what the future configurations of lifelong learning might be.

The retreat atmosphere was exemplary and beneficial for productive dialogue, and AAACE as sponsor, convenor, and fiscal agent was gratified with the result.

The closing of the Retreat on December 1 did not write the final chapter of activity, but instead provided the setting for new alliances, for the reduction of turf battles, and the reduction of proliferations in a field of the education family—adult and continuing education—which often eludes precise definition. The feedback about the retreat has been positive; the retreat format has spirited a frontier for the reaffirmation of working in unison.

If there is one imperative for the future in adult and continuing education, it must be the wise management of our human resources. The 1982 Lifelong Learning Leaders Retreat marshalled together a group of concerned professionals who took steps to sustain and improve the lifelong educational opportunities of adults.

Sponsors—American Assn. for Adult & Cont. Ed. 103

Consultants, Group Facilitators and Staff
Left to Right: Gary A. Eyre, Executive Director, AAACE; Donna M. Gruntz, Director of Membership Services, AAACE; Lloyd Davis, Consultant, AAACE; Thurman White, Vice Chancellor for Outreach, Oklahoma Regents for Higher Education; Herman (Reck) Niebuhr, Associate Vice President and Assistant to the President, Temple University; Ned Lester, Associate Dean, Virginia Polytechnical Institute and State University; Wendell Smith, Dean, Continuing Education-Extension, University of Missouri-St. Louis; Mary Grefe, President of Lead Associates, Ltd. (Des Moines); Everette Nance, Associate Professor of Education Administration and Director, Community Education Development Center, University of Missouri-St. Louis; Ron Gross, Director of the Independent Scholarship Project and Senior Consultant to the College Board (Dr. Gross was the Retreat conference synthesizer and reporter); Michael Doyle, Senior Associate and co-founder of Interaction Associates, Inc. (San Francisco); Roger Hiemstra, Professor and Program Leader—Adult Studies, Syracuse University; Beverly Copeland, Associate Executive Director, AAACE; Pamela Sanfilippo, Administrative Secretary to the AAACE Kellogg Project.

VIII. Follow-Up Plans

Synthesis Team

In June, seven leaders from various associations interested in the education of adults met in Detroit to review progress since the November 1982 Lifelong Learning Leaders Retreat at Airlie House and to explore future directions. The team members included: Gary A. Eyre, Executive Director of the American Association for Adult and Continuing Education and Participant at the Lifelong Learning Leaders Retreat; Mary Grefe, President of LEAD Associates and Facilitator at the Lifelong Learning Leaders Retreat; Alan B. Knox, Division Director of Continuing and Vocational Education for the University of Wisconsin-Madison; Herman (Reck) Niebuhr, Associate Vice President and Assistant to the President for Planning Coordination at Temple University and Consultant at the Lifelong Learning Leaders Retreat; Wendell L. Smith, Dean of Continuing Education-Extension at the University of Missouri-St. Louis and Project Director of the Lifelong Learning Leaders Retreat; Paul Tremper, Executive Director of the National Community Education Association and Participant at the Lifelong Learning Leaders Retreat; Thurman White, Interim Vice Chancellor for Educational Outreach for the Oklahoma State Regents for Higher Education and Consultant at the Lifelong Learning Leaders Retreat; and Arlon Elser, Program Officer of the W. K. Kellogg Foundation.

The progress that has already occurred in the implementation of the Retreat recommendations has been heartening, and evidence of the growing momentum is reported elsewhere in this report.

During the next few months, we will be talking with Retreat participants about further instances of useful collaboration among associations in the field. Late this summer or early in the fall, a small task-planning group will meet to plan Airlie II, to be held this winter.

The task-planning group will review major examples of cooperation among associations and explore emerging issues for further collaboration. These emerging issues will become the agenda for Airlie II. The focus will be on issues that are best addressed through concerted action by various associations. At that time, participants will discuss ways to build support for education of adults and agree on concerted action. Included are ways to build public understanding of lifelong learning by adults, strengthen policy and legislative support, and increase communication among practitioners in various segments of the field. The planning group will be seeking resources and assistance to support these further cooperative efforts.

Collaboration is Arriving

In the spring 1983 Summary Report of the Lifelong Learning Leaders Retreat, a headline question was "Has the Time For Collaboration Arrived?" In the six months that have elapsed since the Airlie House Retreat, there is evidence that the fostering of better acquaintances and association collaboration has been facilitated.

One of the major areas of activity and collaboration is in the legislative arena. With matters of block grants and consolidation, appropriations, authorizing bills, and reauthorizations of both state and federal legislation on the agenda of adult and continuing education groups, working together is a recognized must.

House and Senate committees at the federal level have received testimony on appropriations marked for adult education, vocational education and recommendations for education functions in the fiscal 1984 federal budget. The dialogue generated at Airlie House was a catalytic agent in assisting the coordination of legislation.

Several officers and staff members of associations in attendance at the retreat have met on three occasions to share organizational directions and societal issues which have emerged since the November sessions.

With the release of the report by the National Commission of Excellence in Education entitled, *A Nation at Risk,* and three other reports on defining the problems affecting American education leaders in adult, continuing and community education together with those in retraining programs we are looking quickly to new and better learning models at all levels of education.

The collaborative model of the Airlie House retreat provides a network for addressing the *issues of mediocrity* in education.

Societal issues and concerns impacting on adults have also been given a first examination by several associations and organizations as a result of the retreat.

Future efforts need to focus on leadership seminars and professional development, adult literacy, learner grants under provisions of higher education legislation, high-technology understanding and use, and of major impact, the politics of education in the 1984 state and federal elections.

Through collaborative efforts, associations have the potential to accomplish goals more efficiently and effectively.

Retreat Participants:
Front Row: Wayne Whelan, Thurman White, Harry Allen, George Fellendorf, Edward Scannell, Lowell Eklund, Ned Lester, Harold McAninch, Dale Parnell, Andrew Hansen, Henry Herzing, Joe Mills.
Second Row: Dick Millard, William Barton, Anthony Farma, Sharon Faison, Elizabeth Stone, Dee Brock, Linda Resnik, Retha Clark King, Fran Spinelli, Anne-Marie McCartan, Rawlein Soberano, Carol Stoel, Pam Sanfilippo, Mary Grefe, Gary A. Eyre.
Back Row: Lloyd Davis, Rick Ventura, Paul Braden, Benjamin Massey, William Fowler, Morris Keeton, Gene Whaples, Tom Ridlehuber, Michael Doyle, Paul Tremper, Reck Niebuhr, Ken Young, Wendell Smith, Quentin Gessner, Jerry Miller, Roger Hiemstra, Ron Gross, Rusty Garth, Everette Nancy, Beverly Copeland, Donna M. Gruntz. (Not in photo: David Peoples)

IX. Appendices

A. Retreat Participants

1. **American Assn. for Adult & Cont. Education**
   1201 Sixteenth Street, N.W.;
   Suite 301
   Washington, D.C. 20036
   (202) 822-7866

   Gene Whaples, Co-President

   Tom Ridlehuber, Co-President

   Gary A. Eyre, Executive Director

2. **American Assn. of Community & Jr. Colleges**
   One DuPont Circle, N.W.
   Washington, D.C. 20036
   (202) 293-7050

   Harold McAninch,
   Chairman of the Board

   Dale Parnell,
   President

3. **American Assn. for Higher Education**
   One DuPont Circle, N.W.;
   Suite 600
   Washington, D.C. 20036
   (202) 293-6440

   Anne-Marie McCartan
   Graduate Student

4. **American Council on Education**
   One DuPont Circle, N.W.;
   Suite 801
   Washington, D.C. 20036
   (202) 833-4700

   Jerry W. Miller

   Benjamin Massey

5. **American Library Association**
   50 East Huron
   Chicago, IL 60611
   (312) 944-6780

   Elizabeth Stone

   Andrew M. Hansen

6. **American Soc. for Training & Development**
   600 Maryland Avenue, S.W.;
   Suite 305
   Washington, D.C. 20024
   (202) 484-2390

   Edward Scannell, President

7. **American Vocational Assn., Inc.**
   2020 North Fourteenth Street
   Arlington, VA 22201
   (703) 522-6121

   Joe Mills

8. Association for Continuing Higher Education
   University of Tennessee-Knoxville
   432 Communications Building
   Knoxville, TN 37996
   (615) 974-6629

   Wayne Whelan, Pres. Elect

   William D. Barton,
   Exec. Vice Pres.

9. Coalition of Adult Education Organizations
   Department of Adult Continuing Education
   Montclair State College
   Upper Montclair, NJ 07043
   (201) 893-4353

   Fran M. Spinelli, President

10. Council for Advancement Experiential Learning
    300 Lake Front North
    Columbia, MD 21044
    (301) 596-6799

    Morris Keeton,
    President

11. Council on Postsecondary Accreditation
    One DuPont Circle, N.W.; Suite 760
    Washington, D.C. 20036
    (202) 452-1433

    Reatha Clark King, President

    Richard Millard, President

12. Fund for Improvement of Postsecondary Education
    400 Maryland Ave., S.W.
    ROB Room 3100
    Washington, D.C. 20202
    (202) 245-8099

    Rusty Garth

    Carol Stoel

13. Nat'l Advisory Council on Adult Education
    425 Thirteenth Street, N.W.; Suite 323
    Washington, D.C. 20004
    (202) 376-8892

    Rawlein Soberano, Chairperson

    Rick Ventura, Executive Director

14. Nat'l Advisory Council on Cont. Education
    425 Thirteenth Street, N.W.; Suite 529
    Washington, D.C. 20004
    (202) 376-8888

    Paul Braden

    Lowell Eklund

15. Nat'l Advisory Council/ Vocational Education
    425 Thirteenth Street, N.W.; Suite 412
    Washington, D.C. 20004
    (202) 376-8873

    George Fellendorf

Appendix—Retreat Participants

16. **Nat'l Assn. of Trade and Technical Schools**
    2021 K Street, N.W.
    Washington, D.C. 20006
    (202) 296-8892

    Henry Herzing, President

17. **National Community Education Assn.**
    1201 Sixteenth Street, N.W.;
    Suite 305
    Washington, D.C. 20036
    (202) 466-3530

    Harry Allen, President

    Paul Tremper, Executive Director

18. **National Home Study Council**
    1601 Eighteenth Street, N.W.
    Washington, D.C. 20009
    (202) 234-5100

    David L. Peoples, President

    William A. Fowler, Executive Director

19. **Nat'l University Cont. Education Assn.**
    One DuPont Circle, N.W.;
    Suite 360
    Washington, D.C. 20036
    (202) 659-3130

    Quentin H. Gessner, President

    Kenneth Young, Executive Director

20. **Public Broadcasting Service**
    475 L'Nfant Plaza, S.W.
    Washington, D.C. 20024
    (202) 488-5360

    Dee Brock

    Linda Resnik

21. **United States Assn. of Evening Students**
    Box 308
    Needham Heights, MA 02194
    (617) 237-4418

    Sharon Faison

    Anthony Farma, Executive Director

B. Participant Questionnaire

INSTRUCTIONS: Please indicate your projections concerning change or the significance of each over the next ten (10) years.

I. Demographic Projections:

1. To what extent do you project adult and continuing education enrollments to change in each of the following areas?

	D*	S*	IM*	IC*
A. Non-credit personal enrichment	1	2	16	5
B. Non-credit vocational or skill development		1	8	15
C. Non-credit professional development		3	10	11
D. Credit degree seeking (undergraduate)	3	11	7	3
E. Credit degree seeking (graduate)	5	7	6	6
F. Credit non-degree seeking	5	8	8	3

2. How will the number and scope of each of the following lifelong learning educational providers change?

	D*	S*	IM*	IC*
A. Area vocational schools	1	7	8	8
B. Business and industry inservice programs		1	8	15
C. Colleges and universities	4	8	11	1
D. Junior colleges	2	5	7	10
E. Private trade schools		4	14	6
F. Public secondary schools	7	4	10	3
G. Others (list) *Union training*				1
Community and technical colleges			1	
Community schools				1
Business and industry (trng/dev.)				1
Professional associations				1

Participant Questionnaire

	D	S	IM	IC
3. To what extent will memberships in the following types of professional associations change?				
A. Individual membership based	5	8	10	1
B. Institutional membership based	4	12	8	
C. Association or consortial membership based		9	14	1

*D —Decrease
S —Stay the same
IM—Increase Moderately
IC —Increase Considerably

II. Learning Methods/Locations

1. To what extent will the following learning methods or delivery systems be used?

	D	S	IM	IC
A. Computer assisted learning			7	17
B. Video cassette systems			13	11
C. Video via satellite			8	16
D. Video via cable		1	5	18
E. Audio cassette		6	11	7
F. Audio via radio	5	8	10	1
G. Correspondence study	6	9	7	2
H. Others (list) *video disc*				2
standard lecture		1		

2. To what extent will utilization of the following learning locations likely change?

	D	S	IM	IC
A. Traditional school facilities	3	9	9	3
B. Work location			14	10
C. Home		4	11	9
D. Libraries	2	12	9	1
E. Others (list) *off campus centers*				1
church		1		
military				1
corrections			1	

	D	S	IM	IC
3. Learning scope—To what extent will the traditional focus on cognitive and career related learning be expanded (e.g. value learning, value effective, role learning, other)?	2	4	13	4

III. Financial Concerns

	D	S	IM	IC
1. Participant fees for adult and continuing education programs will . . .		1	16	7
2. Membership fees in professional associations will . . .			21	3
3. What extent will each of the following play in bearing the costs of adult and continuing education?				
Pre-service				
A. The individual student		6	11	7
B. Employers	3	3	13	4
C. Government	12	8	2	
D. Others (list)				
In-Service				
A. The individual student	1	5	12	6
B. Employers		3	11	10
C. Government	13	8	2	1
D. Others (list)				
4. How will your association derive its financial resources?				
A. Membership dues	1	5	10	1
B. Publication sales	2	1	12	
C. Conference registration fees	1	7	6	1
D. Conference exhibit income	2	5	8	
E. Advertising		3	9	
F. Grants and contracts	4	3	7	2
G. Endowments and bequests	1	6	4	1
H. Other (list)		1		

Participant Questionnaire

	D	S	IM	IC
5. How will your association's resource expenditures on each of the following change?				
A. Publications	4	6	9	3
B. Executive staffing	2	11	7	1
C. Legislative relations	1	7	11	1
D. Office facilities	1	11	8	1
E. Others (list) *computer technology*				1
workshops/seminars			1	

IV. Quality Standards/Certification

	D	S	IM	IC
1. Pre-service preparation of professionals to serve the adult and continuing education professions.		7	14	3
2. In-service opportunities for adult and continuing education professionals.		2	17	5
3. The coordination of providers of educational opportunities for adults.		2	19	3
4. Re-licenseur requirements within the professions.	1	10	5	6
5. Accreditation of adult and continuing education programs.		9	12	3
6. The certification of instructors in various adult and continuing education settings.				
A. Adult basic	1	11	9	
B. Industry		9	10	3
C. Private trade		10	8	4
D. Higher education	1	12	10	
E. Others (list) *secondary adult education*			1	
7. Scholarly research regarding the various aspects of adult and continuing education.		3	18	2

V. Issue Identification
1. Ability to secure adequate funding to continue operation.
   Quality control
   Tuition funding
   Increased regulation and external control
   Access and opportunity issues
   Coordination/collaboration
   Attitude issues that must be adopted by those in higher education to accept those in adult education as equals
   Lack of adequate resources
   lack of coordination of different agencies, organizations and institutions that offer the same education programs vis-a-vis the same source of major funding, i.e., the Federal government.
   More effective use of resources; public, private and personal
   Training and educating workers deficient in basic skills
   Finance: what are the best means of financing adult learning.
   How to enable adult learners to pay for (or have paid for) our services
   Illiteracy (increasing impact on society/economy)
   Organization and determination of research data to help service needs
   Financial survival (institutional)
   Economy
   Resources
   Retraining for new careers
   Computer/word-processing technology
   A Federal policy for training and/or re-training the workforce of America to counter unemployment.
   Creating a national blueprint of continuing education that will provide adequate access to resources available to all at any time or place, and gaining universal acceptance of the plan.

Participant Questionnaire 117

2. Identity/identification
   Fiscal support
   Recruiting
   Maintaining quality in increasingly competitive market and more use of technology-based programs
   Quality issues
   Accredibility
   Quality standards
   Financial commitment by state and Federal government must be increased to help adult education
   Competition with private industry in providing training programs
   Decreasing revenues vis-a-vis an increase in the number of people seeking adult education programs
   Competition (related to resources) among providers of education
   Vast differences on a regional basis of the adult retraining needed to be done
   To what extent should the field encourage greater cooperation with the private sector? (Is the current balance between government and non-government sponsorship of adult education the best for our time and circumstances?)
   How to cope with the competition among service providers or to achieve a division of labor among them
   Unemployment
   Marketing the services
   Financing postsecondary education (students)
   Demographics (baby bust)
   Keeping up with state of the art (curriculum)
   Computer literacy
   Education necessary to effect the transition of professionals and non-professionals into high technology jobs to include the training of trainers
   Making effective and wide use of new technologies, i.e. satellite communications, videodisc, etc.

3. Turfdom—the ability to keep from being absorbed by others
   Instructional adaptation to new techniques
   Electronic education—computer assisted, etc.
   Control of academic program proliferation, dealing with pressure to create "applied" programs from cognitive programs
   Telecommunications
   Policy at state and local levels
   Financing
   Education of teachers in higher education to learn how to teach adult students
   Need for more re-training opportunities as jobs become more specialized
   Lack of lobbying body, vis-a-vis that of the vocational education group
   Certification requirements and barriers
   Obtaining sufficient financial support for the individual or institution involved in adult training and education
   What are the best ways to foster increased relationships among adult education associations
   How to improve and expand access to optional learning services for adult learners
   Underemployment
   Improving the image of the professional
   Adaptation to and use of new technologies
   Governmental influence on laws re: training
   Teacher quality
   Training of displaced workers, including homemakers
   Incentive for private sector involvement and the role of higher education institutions in the foregoing
   Ability to provide quality control of continuing education offerings
4. Technological innovations
   Competition among different types of providers
   Qualified and willing faculty
   Interstate delivery of programs, especially using media
   Finance/financing for continuing education (4)
   Technology (2)

Legitimacy
Necessary public relations by those in adult education to let government, higher education, industry, know that adult education can be the answer to many problems
Graying of America
Perception of this Administration as anti-education overall
Government policy—state vs. Federal
Obtaining and instituting a better communication and coordination system among educators, business and government; so a better match between employment needs and education and training can be made
What is the best system of certification, regulation and licensing for the various facets of adult education
How to minimize dysfunctional regulation of service providers
Establishing better relationships with the community, especially the business segment
Expanding access and completion rates to *all* populations
Working cooperatively with other professions

5. Ability to attract and hold good, qualified staff
Adaptation to variety of student clienteles
Cost control
Venture capital for program development, innovation
Business, industry, labor/college relationships, linkages
Jurisdictional
A commitment to encourage adults to lifelong learning by providing an environment for equal education opportunities and quality leadership training as part of the learning process
Are we really reaching those individuals who need us the most —must look at our delivery networks
Negative repercussions of perceived "politicization" of various national advisory councils
Business/industry cooperation with higher education
How to induce adjustment of colleges and universities to the demands of fuller responsiveness to adult learners
High technology; computers, word processing, robotics
Establishing lifelong learning as the American ideal

Adapting to growing competition between postsecondary and other education offering institutions
Liaison between business and education
Integrating resources
Impacting at all levels of the educational hierarchy the cognitive realization of the essentiality of and the neuristic motivation for pursuit of lifelong learning (This should/could be the number 1 issue and objective for all of us)
Motivating people to continue a lifestyle of learning

6. Institutional integrity (i.e., relation to mission, administrative structure, faculty involvement, program coordination and control)
Related to quality control, but involves crucial set of sub-issues

VI. Collaborative Efforts

Please indicate the degree to which you envision the following types of relationships occurring among allied lifelong lifelong learning associations in the next 10 years.

	D	S	IM	IC
1. Meetings of key staff and officers		1	15	6
2. Sharing of staff services (office space, etc.)		6	14	2
3. Collaboration on legislative relations		1	8	14
4. Joint publications		9	11	3
5. Co-sponsorship of research projects		4	15	4
6. Co-sponsorship of regional and theme conferences		1	15	6
7. Jointly conducting annual national conferences		9	10	4
8. Publications exchange				
A. Extended to executive staff		4	15	4
B. Extended on a cost basis to membership		4	17	2
9. Others (list) *personnel exchange*			1	
multi-use of computers				1

C. Retreat Agenda

Monday, November 29, 1982

2:30– 5:30	Administration Planning Meeting*	Tack Rm
4:00– 6:00	Registration and Reception	Lodge
6:00– 8:00	Dinner, Program Overview and Self Introductions, including 3–5 minute reports by each assn. on their association's scope and expectations for the retreat	Meadow Rm; *Airlie Hs*
8:00–10:00	Get Acquainted Hospitality (with cocktails, coffee and dessert)	Meadow Rm; *Airlie Hs*

Tuesday, November 30, 1982

8:00– 9:00	Breakfast	Airlie Rm; *Airlie Hs*
9:00–10:00	Continuation of associations' comments concerning their scope and retreat expectations	*Storeroom*
10:00–11:15	Summary of consultants' papers/questions	*Storeroom*
11:15–11:30	Break	*Storeroom*
11:30–12:15	Four concurrent groups: "Problem Identification"	Tack Rm, Granary Rm, Livery & Hitching Post
12:15–12:30	Plenary voting on priority of problems	*Storeroom*
12:30– 1:30	Lunch	Airlie Rm; *Airlie Hs*
1:45– 2:45	Plenary session. Identification of afternoon/evening concurrent group topics	*Storeroom*
2:45– 3:00	Break	*Storeroom*
3:00– 5:00	Resume concurrent groups	See above
5:00– 6:00	Administration Planning Meeting*	Lake Cottage
6:30– 7:30	Dinner	Ailie Rm; *Airlie Hs*
7:45– 9:30	Concurrent Groups Finalize Recommendations	See above
9:30–11:00	Cocktails, Coffee and Dessert	*Lodge*

Wednesday, December 1, 1982

8:00– 9:00	Breakfast	Airlie Rm; *Airlie Hs*
9:00–10:30	Retreat Wrap-up (Either panel, or closing keynote, or combination.)	Storeroom
10:30–10:45	Break	Storeroom
10:45–11:30	Resume Prior Session	Storeroom
11:30–12:30	Lunch	Federal Rm; *Airlie Hs*
12:30	Adjourn	
12:30– 2:00	Administration Planning Meeting (optional for those whose travel schedules allow.)	Lake Cottage

Retreat participants are shown continuing discussions at one of the informal receptions.

Lowell Elkland and Thurman White

Harold McAnich and Lloyd Davis

D. Evaluation

	Poor	Fair	Good	Excellent

I. Pre-Retreat Information
A. To what extent were you appraised of pre-retreat information regarding:
  1. General intent and purposes of retreat

		5	16	9

  2. Housing and transportation logistics

			14	16

B. To what degree was the questionnaire helpful in your personal analysis of retreat alternatives and your assessment of the views of others?

	2	6	15	4

C. Other Comments:

• The papers arrived very close to my departure for Airlie. Because I represented my national President, I did not complete a questionnaire.

• The pre-conference material should be in hand no later than two weeks prior to assembly. The excellent position papers were not provided sufficiently ahead of time to provide for review.

• More background information on past collaborative attempts would have been useful. Also, a clearer notion of expectations.

• Outstanding staff preparation and hospitality leading up to the program.

	Poor	Fair	Good	Excellent

II. On-Site Facilities and Retreat Coordination

A. How do you rate Airlie Convention facilities and food service

| | 1 | 17 | 13 |

B. How efficient was the on-site retreat registration procedure and other related retreat management

| | 1 | 9 | 21 |

C. To what extent was the agenda organized to maximize the retreat purposes

| | 4 | 16 | 10 |

D. Other Comments:

• Staff not organized for retreat process—markers, tape materials—lost time and motion. Failure to keep on schedule. Not enough time for informed networking and "loose couplings."

• This was an extremely well organized conference . . . and I've attended many.

• Appreciated flexibility in adjusting schedule when seemed appropriate.

• More time and better organized time could be devoted to the concurrent sessions and workshops.

• Looked ideal at outset for (c) above, but didn't sustain effectiveness in the small groups and their work.

• Slight personal reservations on facilities: meals too heavy (but you can't please 'em all)

Evaluation 125

	Poor	Fair	Good	Excellent
III. Retreat Objectives To what extent were the following objectives of the retreat accomplished:				
A. To foster better acquaintance among leaders of lifelong learning associations and organizations		1	11	19
B. To identify major issues which will likely confront lifelong learners and our associations within the next decade		3	12	15
C. To analyze alternatives leading to the resolution of identified issues		9	18	4
D. To formulate recommendations for individual association action and for collaborative efforts between associations	1	8	16	5

E. Other Comments:

• Facilitator allowed group to wander, let several dominate with asides and "show and tell."

• The electronic voting was extremely helpful. Although it would serve no real purpose, it would be interesting to know why individuals did not support some of the issues and recommendations.

• More time needed to identify and analyze the issues, problems, alternatives, etc.

- Additional work needs to be done on (d) above. Assistance/identification of lead agencies for carrying out the recommendations needs further thought. A steering committee from the whole group might develop a timeline and possible action steps to supplement the recommendations.
- Not really enough time for (c) and (d) above.
- Much of this was done; but I was unhappy with the quality of drafts and the vagueness of action plans. Some of us are taking specific steps to get some cooperation going.
- Urgent. Essential—imperative that we follow up and implement.
- To some degree, the follow up will determine success.

IV. Process

How would you rate the utilization at the retreat of each of the following processes in accomplishing our overall goals?

	Poor	Fair	Good	Excellent
A. November 29 opening dinner		5	18	6
B. November 30 plenary session regarding consultants' position papers		3	12	15
C. November 30 concurrent group meetings to identify problems		2	17	10
D. November 30 plenary session to vote on priorities of problems		4	13	12
E. November 30 concurrent group meetings to analyze alternatives to the resolution of issues and to formulate recommendations for action	2	7	13	8

	Poor	Fair	Good	Excellent
F. November 30 cocktail, coffee and dessert hospitality		2	17	11
G. December 1 plenary session panel		2	15	13
H. December 1 closing plenary session		3	17	10

I. Other items

- Too much to do at last session—group proces requires much time, effort and patience, but is ultimately worth it.
- Introductions of facilitators were too long and unnecessary.
- Greater attention should be devoted to pre-conference preparation, i.e. building of agenda, position paper distribution.
- Commissioned papers were particularly useful in setting the stage for discussion.
- Great—really need the follow up meeting.
- Warmth and enthusiasm of retreat leaders carried the day. Doyle, Gross, Roger, especially emerged s dynamic, purposeful leaders, "keep on track, get it done" types.
- National strategy with promotion the essence!
- All of the above.
- The opportunity to get together was major contribution—good for communication. Less than satisfied in terms of building closer, cooperative relationships.
- Created awareness of the other associations. Opportunity for interface was excellent. Education as a whole needs more of this kind of opportunity.
- Useful for future contacts and collaborative efforts. Bottom line will be the follow up and results.
- The concept is great. Alliances were begun that could foster better adult learning.

- Excellent camaraderie and collegiality of participants. The willingness to share resources should open avenues of communication and cooperation. It is important we continue this dialogue.
- Not really. It was interesting and I met some interesting people and learned about various organizations. Mike Doyle's paper was good—excellent, but much of the rest was nebulous. For me it was valuable, but I doubt much will come of it. Sorry!
- Very useful—knowledge of other associations' interests, resources and how we might join together to address common concerns. Might want to consider expanding group to involve more associations with related interest.
- Will serve all of the above.
- Putting "faces" with "names" is extremely useful: facilitates establishing those "loose couplings" so helpful in getting things done.
- Should be a good motivator for action. We need to make sure action actually takes place.
- New contacts. Some joint efforts. A very generalized consensus—to emphasize human resource development.
- Increased awareness of what others are doing (or not doing). Not much else.
- I have learned to appreciate the other aspects of adult education. The conference has provided an opportunity to interface with *all* aspects of adult education and I will now have a better objective and perspective of the wholistic world of adult education. I would hope that whatever we have wrought will come to fruition as it needs to be accomplished.
- Seeking alliances with other associations. Briefing colleagues. Writing. A very worthwhile meeting!
- With Jerry Miller, Dale Parnell, et al., I am working on some joint efforts on public policy. We will use some of the materials in CAEL News. Ken Young is sending a representative to CAEL's January 21, 22 work planning meeting.

- The identification of a national human resources strategy at the "grass roots" level was significant.

- Probably all of the above. I have written reports and evaluation to the NACCE and Kellogg and have sent you copies. Believe they address this question fulsomely. I applaud R. Gross' book idea.

- Increased awareness of other organizations and their activities.

- The experience of the retreat itself may be helpful in our association interacting more closely with other associations in attendance. The "payoff" of the retreat will be progress in implementing recommendations which will certainly necessitate some joint and coordinative efforts.

V. **Impact**

How do you think the experiences of the retreat will be useful to you and your association? (e.g. briefing colleagues, initiating association activities, writing, speaking, publishing, seeking alliances with other associations)

- Developed a few new contacts that can be helpful to our association. Can lead to additional cooperation efforts. The problem will be like similar meetings—follow up. Additionally, the recommendations in some cases were too vague—or promoted motherhood and the flag—hard to disagree with. Excellent process and facilitators and staff.

- Greatly broadened horizons re: other associations and programs of action. Excellent network building opportunities— needed more "down" time for informal meetings.

- Since I am still a "novice" and quite open for suggestions and polishing, I was afforded the opportunity to meet with fascinating persons in the world of education. My association will greatly benefit from my attendance at this retreat because I (and my counterpart) will take back all of the ideas and suggestions. We intend to stay a viable part of this group and hope to be included in future conferences as we are all a part of adult education—learning through life.

- I intend to make sure the information and recommendations are well known in my association. There are several items which will be priority for us. I can see the materials and format useful for a state level.

- In at least all the ways mentioned. Although representatives and officers of the associations of ten come into regular contact with each other, it is important to have a setting and opportunity such as this to brainstorm on how to improve that to which we are all dedicated: opportunities for learners.

- It is uplifting to come across people from diverse organizations from all over the country who work towards the same goals/objectives and to be able to collaborate with them in the future. The weight of this burden (enhancing lifelong learning throughout the nation) becomes light when shared by many.